Interpreting Prophecy

An Essay in Biblical Perspectives

By
PHILIP EDGCUMBE HUGHES

1804

William B. Eerdmans Publishing Company

Copyright © 1976 by William B. Eerdmans Publishing Co.
255 Jefferson Ave. S.E., Grand Rapids, Michigan 49502

Printed in the United States of America

Library of Congress Cataloging in Publication Data

Hughes, Philip Edgcumbe.
Interpreting prophecy.

1. Bible — Prophecies. I. Title.
BS647.2.H78   220.1'5   75-41484
ISBN 0-8028-1630-4

Contents

Interpreting Prophecy

The presence of prophetic writings in the Old Testament needs no demonstration. The Old Testament scriptures were commonly spoken of as falling into two major divisions, the Law and the Prophets or Moses and the Prophets (see, for example, Mt. 5:17; Lk. 16:16, 29; 24:27; Acts 13:15; 28:23); though the mention of the Psalms, by which the poetical writings were designated, as a third main section was not unusual (as in Lk. 24:44). Prophetic passages, however, occur throughout the Old Testament and are not limited to the books of the Prophets. It is only to be expected that many prophecies, and especially those couched in cryptic or symbolic language, should present problems of interpretation; and these problems are intensified by the consideration that biblical prophecy not infrequently has two stages of fulfilment, a proximate or preparatory stage and an ultimate or consummating stage. The New Testament, though it too contains many prophetic passages which present similar problems, stands in relation to the Old Testament as fulfilment does to prediction, or as completion does to promise. Consequently a study of the teaching given in the New Testament concerning the fulfilment of prophecy will shed a clear light on the proper principle of the interpretation and understanding of biblical prophecy.

This method, of interpreting the Old in the light of the New, is manifestly both sound and scriptural, because the Holy Spirit by whom the ancient prophets were moved (2 Pet. 1:21) is the same Holy Spirit who enlightened the minds of the apostles following the pentecostal outpouring (Acts 2:1ff.), bringing to their remembrance the instruction they had received from the Lord himself (see Jn. 14:26; Lk. 24:44ff.). There are many places in the New Testament where the fulfilment of specific prophecies is announced and explained, but above all else there is one focal figure in whom the promises of future blessing uttered through the prophets of old achieve their realization, namely, the incarnate Redeemer, Jesus Christ. "All the promises of God find their Yes in the Son of God, Jesus Christ, whom we preached among you," Paul assures his Corinthian readers (2 Cor. 1:19f.). This points us to a principle of cardinal importance: that the prophetic promises of Holy Scripture are seen in their true perspective only as their light is concentrated on the unique person of him who is the Saviour of mankind and the sole Mediator of all God's covenanted blessings. Thus John the Baptist's father, Zechariah, "filled with the Holy Spirit" declared that the coming of Christ Jesus into this world was the gracious action of God on our behalf, "as he spoke by the mouth of his holy prophets from of old, . . . to perform the mercy promised to our fathers" (Lk. 1:70ff.). Hence the insistence of the apostles that "there is salvation in no one else, for there is no other name under heaven given among men by which we must be saved" (Acts 4:12).

THE FIRST GOSPEL PROMISE

The earliest gospel promise (sometimes called the protevangelium) is found in Genesis 3:15, where God says to the serpent: "I will put enmity between you and the woman, and between your seed and her seed; he shall bruise your head, and you shall bruise his heel." The principle mentioned in the preceding paragraph is well illustrated in this archetypal promise which not only presages, in cryptic terms, the age-long conflict between good and evil but also declares the ultimate victory of Christ over Satan. In Christ Jesus, the eternal Son who through his incarnation became also "the seed of the woman," we have the key to the understanding of this prediction. The bruising of his heel denotes a wound from which he recovers, whereas the bruising of the serpent's head denotes the suffering by Satan of a wound from which there is no recovery. Jesus Christ, whose human descent is traced back to Adam by Luke (Lk. 3:23-38), seemed indeed to have been mortally wounded and totally defeated when he died on the cross and his corpse was laid in the tomb; but it was the wounding only of his humanity, not of his divinity, and the triumph was shown to be his when he rose on the third day from the tomb and subsequently was exalted to the highest glory. At the cross, then, it is Satan not Christ whose head is crushed, for this was God's action for the overthrow of our adversary and the liberation of his creatures (Heb. 2:14f.).

This first gospel promise, therefore, despite the terse and figurative language in which it is expressed, provides a true perspective of the whole sweep of human history. It draws attention to the reality of a cosmic conflict between the will of God and the will of the Devil, between "the seed of the serpent," those who align themselves with the revolt against God, and "the seed of the woman," those who put their trust in the promise of blessing and deliverance. It shows that the outcome of this conflict is not in doubt, that the serpent's head will inescapably be crushed by the promised Saviour, and that the sovereignty of the

11

Creator of all cannot be overturned by the arrogant rebellion of a creature, however exalted he may have been in the hierarchy of creation. It gives the assurance that God's purposes in creation will not be frustrated and brought to nothing but will be carried to completion by the mediation of the promised Seed, through whom God has already ordained "to reconcile to himself all things, whether on earth or in heaven, making peace by the blood of his cross" (Col. 1:20).

The cosmic conflict between the seed of the serpent and the seed of the woman was not limited to the three days bounded by Good Friday and Easter, however; for it was, and is, an age-long conflict of which those three momentous days were the climax. The dreadful intensity of this satanic antagonism to the will of God becomes starkly apparent in the history of the very first children to whom Eve gave birth. Her firstborn son she named Cain, which means "acquisition," looking upon him hopefully, it seems, as the promised deliverer who would crush the enemy's head (Gen. 4:1). But as the boy grew her hopes in him were disappointed, for he aligned himself with the serpent's seed rather than with the posterity of promise, and she gave expression to her disillusionment by calling her second son Abel, which signifies "nothingness" or "vanity" (Gen. 4:2). Yet it was he who truly belonged to the line of faith. And so there follows the first murder, the killing of brother by brother — an act so unnatural, so disruptive of the proper order of creation, that it is plainly an attempt by Satan to sever and obliterate the line that must lead not only to the world's redemption but also to his own doom. Thus from the very earliest times human fellowship has been stultified by the horrible and insensate violence of fratricide, which itself is the evil consequence of rebellion against the goodness of God. Nothing could more graphically depict the spasm of self-destroying hatred

12

by which mankind, in separation from God, is constantly torn and tortured.

The satanic attempt to destroy the line of promise is frustrated, however, by the birth of another son to whom Eve gave the name of Seth, that is "the appointed one," for she looked on him as the one God had appointed in the place of Abel (Gen. 4:25). The fifth chapter of Genesis describes the line of descent which led from Seth to Noah, and the sixth explains the decision of God to send the cataclysmic judgment of the flood because human society had become infected with wickedness to such an appalling degree that the earth was filled with violence and corruption (vv. 5 and 11). But the line of blessing was preserved in Noah, "a righteous man, blameless in his generation," who "walked with God" (v. 9) and who, together with his family, was brought safely through the destruction of the flood in the shelter of the ark (chs. 7 and 8). Thus we see how the enemy's design to eliminate the promised seed by the inundation of the world with depravity was defeated by God's judgment and purging of the world through the inundation of the flood and by his protection of Noah and his family, ensuring the continuity of the good seed until the appearance of the promised deliverer.

And so the conflict persists across the generations of mankind, the enemy constantly striving to overthrow the divine purposes but not succeeding, because God is God and his purposes are sure and cannot fail. But the ways of God are not human ways (Is. 55:8f.). He works his will in the affairs of man by means of the faithful few. In the midst of the rebellious majority there is always God's remnant, so that, throughout the course of human history, it can truly be said: "If the Lord of hosts had not left us a seed, we would have fared like Sodom and been made like Gomorrah" (Rom. 9:29). But in the ultimate issue the will of God is accomplished, not even by a few, but through the medi-

13

ation of the single person of the incarnate Son, who in a unique sense is the promised seed of the woman. He it is who crushes the enemy's head and by his redemptive victory brings all the Creator's purposes to their everlasting fulfilment.

Not that Satan left him unmolested. Quite the contrary: for the appearance of him who is himself the promised seed aroused the enemy to frantic efforts as he sought to subvert the purpose of his coming. Nor was the diabolical assault limited to the confrontation in the wilderness, when Jesus, physically exhausted after forty days without food, overcame the temptations to minister to himself instead of others, to follow an easy road to popular acceptance, and to gain the world at the cost of a single genuflexion, and drove the tempter back with the sword of God's word (Mt. 4:1-11). Rather, it was resumed over and over again throughout the course of his earthly ministry, for example, when Satan, in the voice of Peter, urged him to turn aside from the sufferings and the cross that awaited him in Jerusalem (Mt. 16:21-23), and when, in the voice of his tormentors, even as Jesus was hanging on the cross, he mockingly challenged him to give proof that he was indeed the Son of God by saving himself and coming down from the cross — which again would have meant the defeat of the purpose of his coming, namely, to save others precisely by dying on the cross (Mt. 27:39-43). The incarnate Son, however, was not to be deflected from his determination to fulfil the will of the Father for the redemption of the world. It is by his faithful performance of that will that "we have been sanctified through the offering of the body of Jesus Christ once for all" (Heb. 10:9f.) and that the serpent's head has been crushed; for the purpose of the Son's taking our human nature to himself in his incarnation at Bethlehem was "that through death he might destroy him who has the power of death, that is, the devil, and deliver all those who through fear of

14

death were subject to lifelong bondage" (Heb. 2:14f.).
The cross, where he died in our place, was the instrument whereby "he disarmed principalities and powers and triumphed over them" (Col. 2:15).

GOD'S COVENANT WITH ABRAHAM

The covenant that God made with Abraham was a milestone of the most fundamental importance in the history of prophecy. A right understanding of the significance of the Abrahamic covenant and its implications is conducive to a right understanding not only of the entire prophetic perspective of Holy Scripture but also of the heart of the Christian Gospel itself in which this covenant comes to full fruition. Abraham, the father and founder of the Hebrew nation, was called by God, it will be remembered, before there was any such thing as a chosen nation or a promised land. A citizen of the ancient Chaldean civilization of Ur, he was summoned to set out for an undisclosed destination, showing his firm trust in the divinely given promises by his obedience to the divine command to leave his home and country for a land that God would show him (Gen. 12:1).

To this command was attached a promise of blessing so great that it would extend throughout the whole world; for when God called Abraham in this way he gave him this assurance:

> "I will make you a great nation, and I will bless you, and make your name great, so that you will be a blessing. I will bless those who bless you, and him who curses you I will curse; and by you all the families of the earth will be blessed" (Gen. 12:2f.).

Coupled with the promise of a numerous posterity was the promise that he and his descendants would be the possessors of the land to which God had brought him:

> The Lord said to Abram, after Lot had separated from him, "Lift up your eyes, and look from the place where you are, northward and southward and eastward and westward; for all the land you see I will give to you and to your seed for ever. I will make your seed as the dust of the earth, so that if one can count the dust of the earth, your seed also can be counted" (Gen. 13:14-16).

His posterity would become as innumerable as the stars above:

> Behold, the word of the Lord came to him, ". . . Look toward heaven and number the stars, if you are able to number them." Then he said to him, "So shall your seed be" (Gen. 15:4f.).

The extent of the promised land was also plainly defined:

> On that day the Lord made a covenant with Abram, saying, "To your seed I give this land, from the river of Egypt to the great river, the river Euphrates, the land of the Kenites, the Kenizzites, the Kadmonites, the Hittites, the Perizzites, the Rephaim, the Amorites, the Canaanites, the Girgashites, and the Jebusites" (Gen. 15:18-21).

When Abraham was ninety-nine years old and his wife Sarah still childless God assured him once more that he was to be the father of many nations, confirming this by changing his name significantly from Abram to Abraham and insisting that his covenant with him was an everlasting covenant:

> "I am God Almighty; walk before me, and be blameless. And I will make my covenant between me and you, and will multiply you exceedingly." Then Abram

16

fell on his face; and God said to him, "Behold, my covenant is with you, and you shall be the father of a multitude of nations. No longer shall your name be Abram, but your name shall be Abraham ['father of a multitude']; for I have made you the father of a multitude of nations. I will make you exceedingly fruitful; and I will make nations of you, and kings shall come forth from you. And I will establish my covenant between me and you and your seed after you throughout their generations for an everlasting covenant, to be God to you and to your seed after you. And I will give to you, and to your seed after you, the land of your sojournings, all the land of Canaan, for an everlasting possession; and I will be their God" (Gen. 17:1-8).

The purpose of universal blessing was repeated when the Lord appeared to Abraham by the oaks of Mamre:

The Lord said, "Shall I hide from Abraham what I am about to do, seeing that Abraham shall become a great and mighty nation, and in him all the nations of the earth shall be blessed?" (Gen. 18:17f.).

And again, following the "offering" of Isaac, the son of the promise, Abraham received this reaffirmation:

"By myself I have sworn, says the Lord, because you have done this, and have not withheld your son, your only son, I will indeed bless you, and I will multiply your seed as the stars of heaven and as the sand which is on the seashore. And your seed shall possess the gate of their enemies, and by your seed shall all the nations of the earth be blessed, because you have obeyed my voice" (Gen. 22:15-18).

THE FULFILMENT OF THESE PROMISES

The first stage in the fulfilment of these promises given

to Abraham after he had become a sojourner in the land to which God had led him was the birth of his son Isaac. This in itself was a remarkable event because Abraham was an old man and Sarah his wife was not only long past the age of child-bearing but also had been afflicted with sterility, so that, as Paul observes, it was tantamount to "giving life to the dead and calling into existence things that do not exist." Thus Isaac's birth was manifestly due to the power of Almighty God and at the same time a testimony to the unwavering faith of Abraham in the word that God had spoken:

> In hope he believed against hope that he should become the father of many nations; as he had been told, "So shall your seed be." He did not weaken in faith when he considered his own body, which was as good as dead because he was about a hundred years old, or when he considered the barrenness of Sarah's womb. No distrust made him waver concerning the promises of God, but he grew strong in his faith as he gave glory to God, fully convinced that God was able to do what he had promised (Rom. 4:18-21).

The promise, further, that Abraham's seed would become very numerous and would possess the land of Canaan was also literally fulfilled. The assurance that the land would extend from the Nile to the Euphrates was repeated to Moses — "I will set your bounds from the Red Sea to the sea of the Philistines, and from the wilderness to the Euphrates" (Ex. 23:31) — and in turn to Joshua — "Every place that the sole of your foot will tread upon I have given to you, as I promised to Moses. From the wilderness and this Lebanon as far as the great river, the river Euphrates, all the land of the Hittites to the Great Sea toward the going down of the sun shall be your territory" (Josh. 1:3f.). The conquest of this territory was, however, to be gradual (Ex. 23:29f.), and it was finally accomplished in the reign of Solomon, who "ruled over all the kingdoms

18

from the Euphrates to the land of the Philistines and to the border of Egypt" (1 Kings 4:21). Likewise the prediction of the numerical strength of Abraham's posterity, closely connected as it was with the conquest of the land, came to pass. Thus, shortly before their entry into Canaan, Moses said to the Israelites: "Your fathers went down to Egypt seventy persons; and now the Lord your God has made you as the stars of heaven for multitude" (Dt. 10:22; cf. 1:10). "Therefore from one man, and him as good as dead," says the author of the Epistle to the Hebrews, "were born as many as the stars of heaven and as the innumerable grains of sand by the seashore" (Heb. 11:12). The Israelite was commanded also by Moses that, once he had entered the promised land, he was to acknowledge at the time of the dedication of the firstfruits of his harvest: "I declare this day . . . that I have come into the land which the Lord swore to our fathers to give us. . . . A wandering Aramean was my father; and he went down into Egypt and sojourned there, few in number; and there he became a great nation, great, mighty, and populous" (Dt. 26:3-5).

At the conclusion of the conquest under Joshua's leadership testimony is given to the faithfulness of God in fulfilling all that he had promised: "Thus the Lord gave to Israel all the land which he swore to give to their fathers. . . . And the Lord gave them rest on every side, just as he had sworn to their fathers. . . . Not one of all the good promises which the Lord had made to the house of Israel had failed; all came to pass" (Josh. 21:43-45). So also in David's day the God of Abraham was praised because of the complete trustworthiness of his word:

He is the Lord our God;
  his judgments are in all the earth.
He is mindful of his covenant for ever,
  of the word that he commanded, for a thousand
    generations,

> *the covenant which he made with Abraham,*
> *his sworn promise to Isaac,*
> *which he confirmed to Jacob as a statute,*
> *to Israel as an everlasting covenant,*
> *saying, "To you I will give the land of Canaan*
> *as your portion for an inheritance."*
> . . . .
> *For he remembered his holy promise,*
> *and Abraham his servant.*
> > (Ps. 105:7-11, 42; cf. 1 Chr. 16:7ff.)

Centuries later, Ezra proclaimed on behalf of those who had returned to the promised land from the shame of the Babylonian captivity:

> "Thou art the Lord, the God who didst choose Abram and bring him forth out of Ur of the Chaldeans and give him the name Abraham; and thou didst find his heart faithful before thee, and didst make with him the covenant to give to his seed the land of the Canaanite, the Hittite, the Amorite, the Perizzite, the Jebusite, and the Girgashite; and thou hast fulfilled thy promise, for thou art righteous" (Neh. 9:7f.; see also vv. 9, 23, 25).

Thus we see the clear and emphatic manner in which Moses and Joshua, David and Ezra, not to mention the New Testament writers, bear witness to God's faithful fulfilment of his promise to Abraham that he would be the father of a great nation who would possess the land in which he himself was no more than a stranger and a sojourner (cf. Heb. 11:9).

GOD'S COVENANT WITH DAVID

We shall turn now to another significant milestone in

the prophetic perspective of Holy Scripture, namely, the great promise that God gave to David, to the effect that his would be an everlasting kingdom:

> "The Lord will make you a house. . . . I will raise up your seed after you, who shall come forth from your body, and I will establish his kingdom. He shall build a house for my name, and I will establish the throne of his kingdom for ever. I will be his father, and he will be my son. . . . And your house and your kingdom shall be made sure for ever before me; your throne shall be established for ever" (2 Sam. 7:11-16).

Similarly the psalmist Ethan recites the substance of this covenant promise, when praising God for his "faithfulness to all generations":

> Thou hast said, "I have made a covenant with my
>   chosen one,
>   I have sworn to David my servant:
> 'I will establish your seed for ever,
>   and build your throne for all generations.' "
> . . . .
> "I have found David, my servant;
>   with my holy oil have I anointed him."
> . . . .
> "My faithfulness and my steadfast love shall be
>   with him,
>   and in my name shall his horn be exalted."
> . . . .
> "And I will make him the first-born,
>   the highest of the kings of the earth.
> My steadfast love I will keep for him for ever,
>   and my covenant will stand firm for him.
> I will establish his line for ever
>   and his throne as the days of the heavens."
>   (Ps. 89:3-4, 20, 24, 27-29)

Only in a very partial or minor sense could this promise be said to have been fulfilled in the person of Solomon, David's son who succeeded him as king and

21

built the magnificent temple as a house for God. For one thing, Solomon, as a mere mortal man and a sinner, could not be expected to reign everlastingly; for another, the house that he built was a perishable structure and would in course of time be totally destroyed, as would also be the fate of the one that was built to replace it. As we shall see, the promised king was to build a very different kind of house. The promise to David of a seed through whom a state of blessedness would be established forever recalls, and is indeed a further stage in the fulfilment of, the promise to Abraham that through his seed all the nations of the earth would be blessed. As the seed of both Abraham and David, the promised one must certainly be a man; but as the king who brings everlasting blessing to the whole world he must at the same time be more than man. The expectation is thus aroused that the one to whom the line of the promise leads will be both human and more than human; and the mystery of this double identity is still more graphically propounded by the prophet Isaiah when he writes:

For to us a child is born,
to us a son is given;
and the government will be upon his shoulder,
and his name will be called
"Wonderful Counsellor, Mighty God,
Everlasting Father, Prince of Peace."
Of the increase of his government and of peace
there will be no end,
upon the throne of David, and over his kingdom,
to establish it, and to uphold it
with justice and with righteousness
from this time forth and for evermore.
The zeal of the Lord of hosts will do this.
(Is. 9:6f.)

The statement "a child is born" indicates the true humanity of him of whom the prophet is speaking; but the affirmation "a son is given" signifies something more, namely, that this son is given **by God** — indeed, as we now know, it is **his own son** who is given by God — and his true divinity is confirmed by the divine name by which he is called, including as it does the designation "Mighty God." The fulfilment of this prophecy is achieved, of course, in the divine-human person of Jesus Christ, the Son of God who by virtue of his incarnation became also the Son of Man, the eternal Word who became flesh and dwelt among us (Jn. 1:1-3, 14). To the human descent of Jesus from both Abraham and David the genealogies in the first and third Gospels testify (Mt. 1:1ff.; Lk. 3:23ff.). At the Annunciation, when the angel Gabriel told the Virgin Mary that she was to become the mother of the long-expected Messiah, she was assured, in terms reminiscent of Isaiah 9:6f.:

> *"He will be great, and will be called the Son of the*
> *Most High;*
> *and the Lord God will give to him the throne of his*
> *father David,*
> *and he will reign over the house of Jacob for ever;*
> *and of his kingdom there will be no end."*
>
> (Lk. 1:32f.)

Again, in his Benedictus, Zechariah the father of John the Baptist was inspired to see in the approaching birth of Jesus, of whom John was to be the forerunner, the fulfilment of both the Davidic and the Abrahamic promises. Accordingly he sang:

> *"Blessed be the Lord God of Israel,*
> *for he has visited and redeemed his people,*
> *and has raised up a horn of salvation for us*
> *in the house of his servant David,*
> *as he spoke by the mouth of his holy prophets from*
> *of old,*
> *that we should be saved from our enemies,*
> *and from the hand of all who hate us;*

> *to perform the mercy promised to our fathers,*
> *and to remember his holy covenant,*
> > *the oath which he swore to our father Abraham, to*
> > *grant us*
> *that we, being delivered from the hand of our enemies,*
> > *might serve him without fear,*
> *in holiness and righteousness before him*
> > *all the days of our life."*
> > > (Lk. 1:67-75)

He who is the son of Adam, the son of Abraham, the son of David, and also the Son of God is uniquely qualified not only to sit on the throne of David but also to rule eternally and, by the grace of the redemption he accomplishes, to bring endless blessing to the whole world.

THE COMING OF THE KING

When the king who has been promised comes it is for the purpose of inaugurating his kingdom. Hence the message of his forerunner John the Baptist is, "Repent, for the kingdom of heaven is at hand" (Mt. 3:2). By the kingdom **of heaven** is meant a kingdom that is not this-worldly and that is eternal because it is the kingdom **of God** (Jn. 3:3, 5). The parables of the kingdom concern precisely "the secrets of the kingdom of heaven" (Mt. 13:11). When interrogated by Pilate, Jesus insisted that his kingdom was not of this world: if it had been he and his followers would have resorted to force of arms to establish it (Jn. 18:36). His coming into the world was not for the purpose of engaging in the rivalries and intrigues of human politics but to redeem a people for himself, and the citizens of his

24

eternal kingdom are those who have been ransomed by the blood of his cross (Rev. 5:9f.).

The accomplishment of redemption is followed by the enthronement of the Redeemer. This is the setting up of his kingdom. The author of the Epistle to the Hebrews, for example, asserts that "when he had made purification for sins, he sat down at the right hand of the Majesty on high" (Heb. 1:3) — that is to say, he took his place **on his throne,** the seat of his sovereign authority — and that "we see Jesus, who for a little while was made lower than the angels, **crowned** with glory and honor because of the suffering of death" (Heb. 2:9). In their preaching the apostles emphatically declared that Jesus who had been put to death on the cross was now raised from the dead and exalted and glorified at God's right hand, where he rules as Lord: "Let all the house of Israel therefore know assuredly," Peter proclaimed, "that God has made him both Lord and Christ, this Jesus whom you crucified" (Acts 2:36; cf. 3:13ff.). The incarnate Son fulfilled the purpose of his coming by becoming "obedient unto death, even death on a cross." "Therefore," Paul explains, "God has highly exalted him and bestowed on him the name which is above every name, that at the name of Jesus every knee should bow, in heaven and on earth and under the earth, and every tongue confess that Jesus Christ is Lord, to the glory of God the Father" (Phil. 2:6-11).

From these and similar passages (see Rom. 8:34; Eph. 1:20; Col. 3:1; Heb. 8:1; 10:12; 12:2; 1 Pet. 3:22; Rev. 3:21) it is evident that in the ascension of Jesus to be enthroned in transcendental glory the apostolic writers discerned the fulfilment of the prophetic words with which Psalm 110 opens: "The Lord says to my Lord: 'Sit at my right hand, till I make your enemies your footstool.'" Christ's throne, moreover, is also the throne of those who, redeemed by his blood, are united to him by faith and love. Thus the promise is given to the church in Laodicea: "He who conquers, I will grant him to sit with me on my throne, as I myself conquered and sat down with my Father on his throne" (Rev. 3:21).

It is important to notice that it is as the **incarnate** Mediator, once crucified, now raised and glorified, that the Son sits enthroned at the right hand of God on high. Having assumed our humanity in order that he might redeem it by dying in our place on the cross, he has now exalted that humanity to the glory for which it was originally destined. It is on the Father's throne and at his right hand that the incarnate Son now sits and rules; and there he remains until the end of this age when all human history will be brought to its consummation with the renewal of the whole created order. "The heavens must receive him," Peter says of the ascended Christ, "until the time of universal restoration comes, of which God spoke by his holy prophets" (Acts 3:21). The incarnate Son, therefore, is now removed from this earthly scene, though by reason of the inward working of the Holy Spirit, whom the ascended Saviour sent forth from above, his presence and his power are a great and intimate reality in the experience of the Christian believer.

The return of Christ at the conclusion of this age is "the end," the terminus of all the ages from creation to restoration — not the end of creation or of mankind, but the end in the sense that with the coming of Christ this world will be brought to the glorious destiny for which it was originally formed. It is the end because it means the final judgment of every enemy, the purging from creation of all defilement, and the entry of God's redeemed people into the resplendent fulness of their salvation. This is "the universal restoration" spoken of by Peter. The day of Christ's return will be the end, also, because it will mark the completion of his mediatorial work of reconciliation (2 Cor. 5:18ff.). There is, of course, no suggestion of the end of his kingdom, since it is an everlasting kingdom. Now, however, his mediatorial office fulfilled, he hands over the kingdom to the Father, and so our personal, triune God will be "all in all" in the perfect communion that will evermore prevail between the Creator and his creation. Paul explains what will happen "at his coming," when Christ will raise and glorify "those who belong to him," in the following terms:

> Then comes the end, when he delivers the kingdom to God the Father after destroying every rule and every authority and power. For he must reign until he has put all his enemies under his feet. The last enemy to be destroyed is death. "For God has put all things in subjection under his feet." . . . When all things are subjected to him, then the Son himself will also be subjected to him who put all things under him, that God may be all in all (1 Cor. 15:24-28).

The destruction of death, the last enemy, means the annulment of the evil consequences of sin (Rom. 5:12; 6:23) and the establishment of the new heaven and the new earth in which the former things have passed away and death shall be no more (Rev. 21:1-4).

The apostolic perspective of the New Testament, then, sees Jesus enthroned on high in glory from the time of his ascension until his manifestation at the end of this age, when he will transform his faithful servants into his own likeness and execute final judgment on the impenitent (Rom. 8:29; 1 Cor. 15:49; 2 Cor. 3:18; 1 Jn. 3:2; Acts 17:31; Jn. 3:36; Rom. 2:8; Eph. 5:6; Col. 3:6). His kingdom is not future, but present, extending from his ascension to his return, when he will hand it over to God the Father as universal righteousness is established under the sovereign sway of the trinitarian Godhead. Then at last, when all things have been made new, "the creation itself will be set free from its bondage to decay and obtain the glorious liberty of the children of God" (Rom. 8:21). The conclusion that the risen and ascended

Saviour is even now reigning as king is confirmed by the striking fact that the announcement, "The kingdom of heaven is at hand," so characteristic of the Gospels (see, for example, Mt. 3:2; 4:17; 10:7), is not once found in the Acts and Epistles. The reason for this, as we have shown above, is that, as the apostles consistently taught, the ascension of Jesus denotes also his enthronement and the inauguration of his kingdom. Ruling now as King, he is "the Lord of all" who "bestows his riches upon all who call upon him" (Rom. 10:12). Accordingly, in fellowship with believers of every age, we now joyfully affirm that "God has delivered us from the dominion of darkness and transferred us to the kingdom of his beloved Son" (Col. 1:13).

LIVING IN THE LAST DAYS

In harmony with this perspective, this present age, which was introduced by the first coming of Christ and will be terminated by his second coming, is viewed as the final period of human history prior to the divine restoration of all things (Acts 3:21). Preaching on the Day of Pentecost, Peter declared not only that David (in Ps. 16:8ff.) "foresaw and spoke of the resurrection of the Christ," but also that the risen Jesus, now "exalted at the right hand of God," had "received from the Father the promise of the Holy Spirit" and had sovereignly granted the outpouring of blessing of which his hearers were witnesses (Acts 2:22-36), in fulfilment of the ancient prophecy of Joel that "in the last days" God would pour out his Spirit on all flesh (Joel 2:28ff.; Acts 2:16ff.). According to the apostolic understanding, therefore, the present period is the period of "the last days" predicted by the prophets. These are the last days, also, because God has now through the redeeming mission of his Son spoken his full and final word to mankind, thereby marking this as the end-time (Heb. 1:1f. — "in these last days he has spoken to us by a Son"). By that conclusive word every man will be either eternally saved or eternally judged (Jn. 12:46-48); for its perfection is such that there is nothing that can be added to it. The all-sufficiency of the incarnate Son's atoning sacrifice necessarily means that it has been offered once for all. "By a single offering he has perfected for all time those who are sanctified"; no other offering can be expected (Heb. 10:14-18). That is why Christ (no longer "standing" to offer further sacrifice), "when he had offered for all time a single sacrifice for sins, **sat down** at the right hand of God, then to wait until his enemies should be made a stool for his feet" (Heb. 10:11-13).

The same writer affirms that Christ "has appeared once for all **at the end of the ages** to put away sin by the sacrifice of himself," adding that, "having been once offered to bear the sins of many, he will appear a second time, not to deal with sin but to save those who are eagerly waiting for him" (Heb. 9:26, 28). Similarly, Peter, reminding his readers that they have been redeemed with the precious blood of Christ, explains that "he was destined before the foundation of the world but was made manifest **at the end of the times** for your sake" (1 Pet. 1:18-20). James upbraids those who grow rich through callous rapacity and disregard of the needy, informing them of the ominous truth that they "have laid up treasure **in the last days.**" At the same time he encourages his fellow Christians to be patient and steadfast, "for the coming of the Lord is at hand," and warns grumblers that "the Judge is standing at the doors" (Jas. 5:3, 8, 9). In these last days, then, it is no longer the kingdom of heaven but the coming of the King that is at hand. John even calls this **"the last hour"** (1 Jn. 2:18). The Judge who is standing at the doors is the King already crowned with glory and honor at the right hand of the Majesty on high. It is **the Lord** whose return is imminent.

WERE THE APOSTLES MISTAKEN?

It has been suggested that the apostles were mistaken in their belief that they were living in the last days, that they either misread the signs of the times or even were misguided in thinking that Christ would return at all, and that in any case their hope has proved vain because of the failure of the Lord to come as they expected. John, for example, felt justified in calling it the last hour because the spirit of antichrist was clearly active in the world and in the church when he was writing (1 Jn. 2:18ff.; 4:1ff.). But the sceptics have failed to understand an important element in the perspective of the New Testament, namely, the emphasis on the impossibility of predicting the precise day and hour when the culminating event will take place. The Lord's return may be soon or it may be long delayed. In each succeeding generation the presence of antichrists has been, and continues to be, readily discernible. The coming of Christ, therefore, is **always imminent** and there is need for **constant watchfulness.**

This explains why the prophetic teaching of the New Testament is consistently presented with a strong **ethical** emphasis. It is intended, not as pabulum for mystery-mongers and puzzle-solvers, but as an incentive to godly living. Such instruction is always accompanied by the call to be diligent and watchful in the Master's service, so that when, suddenly, he comes we may not be found wanting. Typical is the following admonition uttered by Christ himself:

> "*Take heed, watch;* for you do not know when the time will come. It is like a man going on a journey, when he leaves home and puts his servants in charge, each with his work, and commands the doorkeeper to be on the watch. *Watch therefore—for you do not know when the master of the house will come,* in the evening, or at midnight, or at cockcrow, or in the morning—lest he come suddenly and find you asleep. *And what I say to you I say to all: Watch!"* (Mk. 13:33-37).

Paul stirs up the Christians in Rome with this challenging appeal:

> You know what hour it is, how *it is full time now for you to wake from sleep.* For salvation is nearer to us now than when we first believed; *the night is far gone, the day is at hand.* Let us then cast off the works of darkness and put on the armor of light; *let us conduct ourselves becomingly as in the day,* not in revelling and drunkenness, not in debauchery and licentiousness, not in quarreling and jealousy. But put on the Lord Jesus Christ, and make no provision for the flesh, to gratify its desires (Rom. 13:11-14).

John urges his readers to live lives befitting those whose Master may appear at any moment:

> Now, little children, *abide in him, so that when he appears we may have confidence and not shrink from him in shame at his coming.* . . . Beloved, we are God's children now; it does not yet appear what we shall be, but we know that when he appears we shall be like him, for we shall see him as he is. *And every one who thus hopes in him purifies himself as he is pure* (1 Jn. 2:28; 3:2f.).

This present fallen world, says Peter, is "being kept

31

until the day of judgment and destruction of ungodly men" (2 Pet. 3:7). In the light of this knowledge, and as all history moves on inexorably to that destined day, our conduct should be marked by urgency and seriousness:

> The day of the Lord will come like a thief, and then the heavens will pass away with a loud noise, and the elements will be dissolved with fire, and the earth and the works that are upon it will be burned up. Since all these things are thus to be dissolved, *what sort of persons ought you to be in lives of holiness and godliness, waiting for and hastening the coming of the day of God,* because of which the heavens will be kindled and dissolved, and the elements will melt with fire! But according to his promise we wait for new heavens and a new earth in which righteousness dwells. Therefore, beloved, since you wait for these, *be zealous to be found in him without spot or blemish, and at peace* (2 Pet. 3:10-14).

As it was in the days of the apostles, so in each succeeding generation the expectation of the Lord's return has been a spur to earnest Christian living. "The sword of the Lord will come soon and swiftly over the earth," proclaimed Savonarola from the pulpit of the Duomo in Florence in 1495.

> Believe me that the knife of God will come and soon. And do not laugh at this word 'soon', and do not say that it is 'soon' as used in the Apocalypse, which takes hundreds of years to come. Believe me that it will be soon. Believing does not harm you at all, as a matter of fact it benefits you, for it makes you turn to repentance and makes you walk in God's way; and do not think that it can harm you rather than benefit you. Therefore believe that it is soon, although the precise time cannot be given, for God does not wish it, so that his elect may remain always in fear, in faith, and in charity, and continually in the love of God.

32

WHY IS CHRIST'S RETURN DELAYED?

Even though the writers of the New Testament plainly teach what had first been learned from Christ himself, namely, that the date of his return is unknown to all except the Father (Mk. 13:32f.; Acts 1:6f.), it cannot be denied that this event, so confidently predicted by the apostles, seems to have been long delayed. The centuries succeed each other and in each generation Christians look expectantly for his appearing, but still he has not come. Does not this open the door for scepticism? Peter addresses himself to this very question in his second epistle, in a passage where he warns his readers that scoffers will arise and will scornfully ask: "Where is the promise of his coming? For ever since the fathers fell asleep, all things have continued as they were from the beginning of creation" — an attitude reflecting the naturalistic mentality which supposes that the world functions without change and without end in accordance with its own built-in laws. Such persons, however, deliberately (and therefore culpably) ignore certain facts, says Peter (2 Pet. 3:3ff.).

In the first place, they ignore the testimony of history, which shows that the predictions of God's prophets, though fulfilment may have been delayed, have not failed to come to pass. A striking and apposite example of this is the preaching of Noah, whose warning of the coming judgment of the flood fell on deaf ears and whose building of the ark in preparation for this event was to the accompaniment of the mocking taunts of his scornful generation. Nevertheless, at God's appointed time the world of his day was destroyed by water, and all the scoffers perished though the coming of the flood had been long "delayed." By a similar word of God, Peter declares, "the heavens and earth that now exist have been stored up for fire, being kept until the day of judgment and destruction of ungodly men." As surely as the judgment by water took place, so surely will the judgment by fire take place.

Secondly, they are mistaken in imagining that things are to be measured by the yardstick of human experience. It is God, not man, who is the Lord of creation and who as such controls all things in accordance with his will and purpose. To judge things, and not least the divine timetable for the future, by merely human standards is therefore foolish. What may seem a very long time to man is as nothing to God. Peter accordingly advises his readers not to overlook this fact, "that with the Lord one day is as a thousand years, and a thousand years as one day." Seen in the light of eternity, any number, whether one or a million, is equally small and insignificant, and consequently we can speak of "delay" only from the limited point of view of man.

Thirdly, they fail to appreciate the fact that the apparent delay in the return of Christ is indicative not of weakness or indecision on God's part but rather of his patience and longsuffering as he gives opportunity for the message of the Gospel to be proclaimed throughout the whole world. "The Lord is not slow about his promise as some count slowness," writes Peter, "but is forbearing toward you, not wishing that any should perish, but that all should reach repentance." The prolongation of this final age is at the same time the prolongation of the day of grace. Those, therefore, who have not come to faith should interpret the "delay" gratefully as a sign of divine goodness which extends to them the opportunity to repent and believe, not scornfully as a sign of divine incompetence.

As this is an era of opportunity for those who do not know the grace of God in Christ Jesus, so also it is an era of evangelism for those who by that grace have become followers of Christ. God freely grants salvation to all, without distinction, who call upon him.

"No one who believes in him will be put to shame," Paul, citing Isaiah 28:16, tells the Christians in Rome. All distinctions of nationality, class, or color disappear in the presence of this radical, universal need of mankind. All are sinners (Rom. 3:23; 5:12); therefore all need the Gospel. "There is no distinction between Jew and Greek," Paul continues; "the same Lord is Lord of all and bestows his riches upon all who call upon him. For 'every one who calls upon the name of the Lord will be saved'" (now quoting Joel 2:32; cf. Acts 2:21). But to call upon the Lord people must believe in him; and to believe in him they must hear about him; and to hear they must have a preacher; and therefore it is necessary that preachers be sent with the message (Rom. 10:11-15). Hence the command of the Master to his disciples to be his witnesses, in the power of the Holy Spirit, to the very ends of the earth. This is the benefit of the "delay" in Christ's return. But it is not at all a delay in judgment. On the contrary, for those who spurn the message of the Gospel there remains only "a fearful prospect of judgment" — fearful because "it is a fearful thing to fall into the hands of the living God" (Heb. 10:27, 31).

THE SAME DAY ONE OF JUDGMENT
AND SALVATION

From the passage 2 Peter 3:10-14 (quoted above, on page 32) it is evident that **the day of the Lord** will be a day of fiery judgment which brings destruction on the ungodly. But it is this same day for which Christian believers are looking. Its approach, therefore, is an incentive to them to live holy and godly lives as they "wait for and earnestly desire the coming of the day of God" when the world will be purged with fire. It will not, of course, be a day of destruction for the Christian believer; if it were, he could hardly be encouraged to desire it earnestly! Before the judgment descends he will be taken to the Lord's presence — as Christ taught, "one will be taken and the other left" (Lk. 17:34f.) — and thus what he looks for is not death but life, not the old world but the new, the purified and restored creation in which righteousness dwells for all eternity. That purifying power he has already experienced in his own heart through the cleansing of Christ's blood and the sanctifying influence of the Holy Spirit; for he is already a citizen of this new world (Eph. 2:19; Phil. 3:20), and in anticipation of its ultimate disclosure he strives, with the help of God's grace, to advance in likeness to Christ so that he may be "found by him without spot or blemish, and at peace."

This perspective, in accordance with which history is now moving toward its consummation in the final day of Christ's return, the day that at the same time will be the day of doom for the godless and the day of glorification for God's redeemed people, is in complete harmony with the teaching of Christ in the Gospels and of the other apostolic authors of the New Testament. Christ, for example, insisted that the events of his final, and still future, coming were prefigured by the days of God's visitation in Noah's time, when those who had entered the ark were preserved, while the unrepentant were overwhelmed by the flood, and in Lot's time, when Lot and his family were rescued while judgment rained down from heaven on the city of Sodom:

> "As it was in the days of Noah, so will it be in the days of the Son of man. They ate, they drank, they married, they were given in marriage, *until the day when*

36

Noah entered the ark, and the flood came and destroyed them all. Likewise as it was in the days of Lot—they ate, they drank, they bought, they sold, they planted, they built, but *on the day when* Lot went out from Sodom fire and brimstone rained down from heaven and destroyed them all—so will it be *on the day when* the Son of man is revealed" (Lk. 17:26ff.; similarly Mt. 24:37ff.).

The great consummating day of the Lord, which will bring this final age to its conclusion, will be a day of salvation for some and a day of destruction for others: it is, clearly, one and the same day.

Similarly, in the vision given to John on the island of Patmos, God is praised because "the time for the dead to be judged" is the time both "for rewarding thy servants, the prophets and saints, and those who fear thy name, both small and great," and "for destroying the destroyers of the earth" (Rev. 11:17f.). No less plain is the teaching of Paul that the day "when the Lord Jesus is revealed from heaven" will not only be the day when he "inflicts vengeance upon those who do not know God and upon those who do not obey the gospel of our Lord Jesus," but will also be the day when he comes "to be glorified in his saints and to be marvelled at in all who have believed," granting them rest from their affliction (2 Thess. 1:7-10). The same day that brings final judgment on the wicked brings the fulness of redemption for God's people. For the former it means "sudden destruction" and "there will be no escape." "But you are not in darkness, brethren, for that day to surprise you like a thief," Paul says to the Thessalonian Christians. For those whose security is in Christ it is no day of doom but, on the contrary, a day of rejoicing: "For God has not destined us for wrath, but to obtain salvation through our Lord Jesus Christ, who died for us so that whether we wake or sleep we might live with him" (1 Thess. 5:2-10).

37

WHAT DID ABRAHAM EXPECT?

We have already seen how the promises that Abraham would be the founder of a great nation and that his posterity would possess the promised land within clearly defined boundaries were precisely fulfilled, and were acknowledged to have been fulfilled, in the subsequent history of Israel. But there was undoubtedly more to the covenant made with Abraham than the counting of heads and the settlement of a particular territory. There is nothing unduly remarkable in the notion of a man's name living on in the generations of his family that succeed him. The promises certainly intended far more than this, for they included the assurance that he, as well as his posterity, would be blessed and would receive the land of Canaan as an everlasting possession, and, moreover, that through his seed all the nations of the earth would be blessed (Gen. 17:1ff.; 22:15ff.). The question inevitably arises: What did Abraham himself expect from these promises? What sort of fulfilment did he himself look forward to?

The need for an answer becomes all the more acute when we remember that the land of promise was like a foreign country to him, in which he and his family lived like exiles under the flimsy shelter of tents, so that he himself could hardly have been said to possess it (Heb. 11:8f.; Acts 7:5). Even in his old age he had to negotiate with the Hittites for the purchase of a piece of land where he could bury his wife Sarah: "I am a stranger and a sojourner among you," he said to them; "give me property among you for a burying place, that I may bury my dead out of my sight" (Gen. 23:4; cf. Acts 7:16). In a territory so alien, and an environment so frequently hostile, how could he believe himself to be blessed by God in respect of the land to which he had come? Indeed, even taking the long view of things, how could he imagine an everlasting blessing to be attached to any portion of this earth which in the nature of the case is not eternal and which, in the apostolic perspective, as we have seen, is destined for fiery judgment? How, then, did he understand the promise of an "everlasting possession" (Gen. 17:8)?

"Do not love the world or the things in the world," admonishes John. "If any one loves the world, love for the Father is not in him. For all that is in the world, the lust of the flesh and the lust of the eyes and the pride of life, is not of the Father but is of the world. And the world passes away, and the lust of it; but he who does the will of God abides for ever" (1 Jn. 2:15-17). This admonition might equally well have come from Abraham himself, for if there was one thing he learned in the land of promise it was not to love the world, not to concentrate his affection on temporal things, but to do the will of God and thus to abide forever. The words used by Paul would have been equally appropriate on Abraham's lips: "I look not to the things that are seen but to the things that are unseen; for the things that are seen are transient, but the things that are unseen are eternal" (2 Cor. 4:18). What was said of Moses by another apostolic author was no less true of Abraham, namely, that "he endured as seeing him who is invisible" (Heb. 11:27). Why? because Abraham's perspective was not this-worldly but next-worldly.

Sustained by a vital faith in God and his word, Abraham willingly endured the hardships by which he was beset in the land of promise, because all along "he looked forward to the city which has foundations, whose builder and maker is God" (Heb. 11:9f.). But not only did Abraham and his family learn to **live by faith;** they also learned to **die in faith,** for when they came to the end of their earthly life "they had not received what was promised." Far from dying in disillusionment, however, their hope remained unshaken as they "acknowledged that they were strangers and exiles on the earth" and so were able to "see and greet" the fulfilment of the promise "from afar." These willing strangers and exiles "make it clear that they are seeking a homeland." But Abraham had left his earthly homeland and the renowned civilization of Ur. Had he desired a homeland of this world he would have been better advised to return to the country he had left, and there was every opportunity for him to do so. But the apostolic writer assures us that he and those with him desired **"a better country, that is, a heavenly one,"** which is precisely what God intended as the focus of their faith and hope. Consequently, the writer adds, "God is not ashamed to be called their God, for he has prepared for them a city" (Heb. 11:13-16). That city is "the city of the living God, the heavenly Jerusalem," and its citizens are the great company of "the first-born who are enrolled in heaven" (Heb. 12:22f.).

The lesson for us, as for Abraham and all men and women of faith, is that **"here we have no lasting city"**; and so, like them, **"we seek the city which is to come"** (Heb. 13:14), the Jerusalem which is above and which is free (Gal. 4:26), realizing that, like all true pilgrims, we are strangers and exiles on the earth because "our citizenship is in heaven," as Paul reminded the Christians in Philippi (Phil. 3:20). Abraham's attention, accordingly, was by no means concentrated on that which is immediately perceptible to the physical senses but rather on a homeland which does not belong to this present order of things and on a city which is eternal because it is built by God — of this his willingness to continue dwelling in tents, the most impermanent and insecure of shelters, gave striking witness.

It has been well remarked (by Calvin) that if the holy patriarchs expected a happy life from the hand of God — as they undoubtedly did — they had in view a different happiness from that of an earthly life. So it has been with all God's true servants throughout the ages. "Seek the things that are above, where Christ is seated at the right hand of God," Christian believers are exhorted. "Set your minds on things that are above, not on things that are on earth" (Col. 3:1f.). Paul, whose life as an apostle was one of severe hardship and persecution, declared: "I consider that the sufferings of this present time are not worth comparing with the glory that is to be revealed to us" (Rom. 8:18). Indeed, any affliction of the present, however intense and prolonged, is but "slight and momentary" when we remember that it is leading us to "an eternal weight of glory beyond all comparison" (2 Cor. 4:17). The gaze of faith penetrates beyond the visible present to the as yet invisible but eternal reality. We who believe are, like Abraham and his company, aliens and exiles in this world (1 Pet. 2:11). In a certain sense we too, like Abraham and his family, dwell in tents, the frail abode of our mortal bodies, but with this assurance: "that if the present earthly tent we live in is dismantled [at death], we have a building from God, a house not made with hands, eternal in the heavens," and that "he who has prepared us for this very thing is God, who has given us the Spirit as a guarantee" (2 Cor. 5:1, 5).

THE SACRAMENTAL PERSPECTIVE

In view of the plain teaching of the New Testament that Abraham's hope was fixed on something far more than a mere this-worldly fulfilment of the promises God made to him, in fact that he looked with confidence for their realization in eternal and heavenly, or next-worldly, blessing which will transcend to an infinite degree all that this present world has to offer, we may conclude that the land to which was attached the prom-

41

ise of an everlasting possession held for him a **sacramental** significance. Despite this promise, God (as Stephen reminded the members of the Sanhedrin before whom he was arraigned) "gave him no inheritance in it, not even a foot's length" (Acts 7:5). In the promised land he learned how partial and ephemeral is any enjoyment that this finite and transitory world affords; but he also learned to see in the land of promise a pointer to that transcendental reality of joy and peace for which every human heart has a longing. He discerned, in other words, that the promise portended far more than the passing fashion of this world can supply. This is what is meant by saying that the land had sacramental significance for Abraham.

Sacraments are defined (in part) in the Second Helvetic Confession as

> mystical symbols or holy rites or sacred actions, ordained of God himself, consisting of his word, of outward signs, and of things signified . . . whereby he seals his promises, and outwardly represents and as it were offers to our sight those things which inwardly he performs for us, and so strengthens and increases our faith through the working of God's Spirit in our hearts (ch. 19).

Briefly, then, a sacrament consists of "the word, the sign, and the thing signified." The sign is not an end in itself, but it points, as any true sign must, to a reality beyond itself. Thus Abraham did not view the earthly territory to which God's promise was attached as an end in itself, but understood it, sacramentally, as a sign pointing beyond itself to a distant and transcendental reality. He saw and greeted the fulfilment of the promise from afar as his gaze of faith penetrated beyond all earthly values to that eternal and heavenly country which is the true homeland of God's people (Heb. 11:13ff.).

The same sacramental perspective belongs, for

example, to the Christian sacrament of the eucharist or Lord's supper (though it would be wrong to imagine that Abraham's sacramental perception was not, by anticipation, essentially Christian, for, as we shall find, he foresaw Christ as the one on whom the light of the covenant promises was focused and in whom they would achieve their fulfilment). When, in the upper room, Christ handed his apostles bread and wine with the words, "This is my body which is broken for you" and "This is my blood of the covenant which is poured out for many," it is obvious that the apostles could not have understood these words in a literalistic sense, for Jesus was physically present with them. Such words could have been accepted literalistically only if he had given them, not bread and wine, but sections from the flesh and blood from the arteries of his own physical body there before them. The significance of the words, however, is sacramental. When conjoined with the words uttered by Christ, the bread and the wine point significantly to a spiritual reality beyond themselves and become to the believing recipient a means of appropriating that grace of which they are signs and pledges — the grace that flows from the cross where Christ's body was broken and his blood shed for the forgiveness of our sins.

In coming to the eucharist we do not come for a physical meal. We come, rather, that in our hearts and by faith we may feed upon Christ and drink his blood, and thus experience and express that we are one with Christ and he with us. The sign to which the promise is annexed conducts us to the supreme reality of blessing which this world can neither give nor take away. So also the New Testament makes it clear that Abraham and the other patriarchs did not seek in the physical land of Canaan their everlasting possession or interpret in a carnal manner the good things promised by God. Had they done so, they would have been bitterly disillusioned men. But the land of promise was an

43

earthly sign pointing beyond itself to a heavenly reality, a pledge of the faithfulness of the promise concerning an everlasting inheritance, and a means to the inward experience even during this present pilgrimage of the blessings it portended. The patriarchs' perspective penetrated far beyond the circumstances of this world to the enjoyment of an eternal state which, though hidden from the physical gaze, is absolutely real to the eye of faith.

THE DISTINCTION BETWEEN THIS WORLD AND THE NEXT

At this point in our discussion it seems appropriate to pause and explain what is meant — and what is not meant — by the distinction between this world and the world to come. This distinction is often expressed in terms of a differentiation between the earthly and the heavenly, or the temporal and the eternal. What is indicated by such language is a great qualitative contrast between life as we now know it and life as it will be known hereafter by the redeemed people of God. There is certainly no implication that the world is in itself evil. After all, it is **God's** world. Therefore the whole order of creation is **good**, in fact **very good** (Gen. 1:31). Any suggestion, therefore, of a dualism of matter and spirit, such as was characteristic of the Greek philosophy stemming from Pythagoras and of the heresy of gnosticism by which the Christian faith was early threatened, is completely out of place; for to postulate that matter is an evil principle and that spirit is a good principle leads inevitably to a denial of the goodness of creation because of its materiality, and re-

44

quires the rejection of such central doctrines as the incarnation of the Divine Son, his atoning suffering and death, and his bodily resurrection and ascension.

The incarnation, indeed, testifies powerfully to the genuine goodness of the human body in particular and of matter in general, and the purpose of the incarnation, fulfilled in the physical death, resurrection, and glorification of Jesus Christ, demonstrates that salvation does not mean the liberation of the spirit from the prison-house of the body, but the redemption of man in the full integrity of his created being, body as well as spirit. The biblical distinction between this world and the next, then, is not at all a dualistic distinction; and, even though no words can possibly describe the incomparable wonder of the inheritance which awaits God's people — for "no eye has seen, nor ear heard, nor the heart of man conceived, what God has prepared for those who love him" (1 Cor. 2:9; cf. Is. 64:4) —, yet the distinction does not imply a discontinuity between this world and the next, but rather the fulfilment of all that God intended in and by his work of creation.

The world, good in itself though it is, labors under the curse that man's sin has brought on things. The goodness of creation has been marred and perverted by the ungodliness of men, with the result that falsehood and hatred and corruption and violence cover the face of the earth. Paul even speaks of creation as "waiting with eager longing for the revealing of the sons of God" when the created order "will be set free from its bondage to decay and obtain the glorious liberty of the children of God" (Rom. 8:19ff.). The new heaven and the new earth of the prophetic vision designate all creation restored to its first beauty and brought to the glorious destiny for which it was designed. Hence the contrast between this present earthly scene and the glory that is yet to be revealed. The apostolic admonition not to love the world does not

45

imply, therefore, the denial of the goodness of creation or of matter, but the renunciation of the fallen values of the world, the loveless lust and the selfish pride and the idolization of material possessions, which stifle the love of God in men's hearts (1 Jn. 2:15f.).

Precisely the same is true of the distinction between the temporal and the eternal. It is not meant to suggest that there is anything bad about time itself, which is the measure of the eventfulness of existence. But, again, in our present state of fallenness time takes on a hostile appearance, for while it marks birth and development for every person it also marks aging and death for every person, and the terminus to which it is inexorably leading is that of final judgment. Thus instead of being the measure of joyful achievement time has become the measure of frustration and futility, and "the span of our years is but toil and trouble" (Ps. 90:10). We should well understand the need for Christ's coming in order that, through his incarnation and death, "he might deliver all those who through fear of death were subject to lifelong bondage" (Heb. 2:15). Christ has overthrown this tyranny of time, and to those who will hear he says: "Fear not, I am the first and the last, and the living one; I died, and behold I am alive for evermore" (Rev. 1:17f.). The Christian who has experienced the new birth into that endless life unshadowed by death knows two things: first, that "the world passes away, and the lust of it"; and secondly, that "he who does the will of God abides for ever" (1 Jn. 2:17).

But it is the world in its fallenness which, ripe for judgment, is passing away, not the world in its createdness as coming from the hand of God. It is in the former sense that "heaven and earth will pass away" (Mt. 24:35), and it is in the latter sense that "we wait for new heavens and a new earth in which righteousness dwells" (2 Pet. 3:13) — a restored creation, in other words, continuous with the present created order, but

purged from all sin and defilement and gloriously transformed by the power and presence of God. No longer
will "earthly" describe a state of fallenness and "heavenly," by contrast, the transcendent holiness of God,
for then earth and heaven will be united in a harmony
of praise and service under the gracious perfection of
God's rule and "all shall know him from the least to
the greatest" (Heb. 8:11; Jer. 31:34). It is important
to notice, therefore, that earth has a place, not only in
this present world, but also in the world to come.

THE CHILDREN OF ABRAHAM

The descendants of Abraham became very numerous,
as God had said they would. God had also promised,
however, that by his seed all the nations of the earth
would be blessed (Gen. 22:18). That this did not mean
that all who could claim Abraham as their forefather
would for that reason be favored by God and acceptable
to him is evident from the history of the people of
Israel. The context of blessing is faith in God's word
and obedience to his will. This was so with Abraham
himself, who, we are told, "believed the Lord, and he
reckoned it to him as righteousness" (Gen. 15:6). As
later developments showed, unfaithfulness brought
dire judgment, instead of blessing, on both the chosen
people and the promised land. The mere fact that they
were descendants of Abraham gave them no privilege
of immunity from the wrath of God. Of this, in fact,
Moses gave them solemn warning as they were preparing to enter the land of promise:

> "Take heed to yourselves, lest you forget the covenant
> of the Lord your God, which he made with you. . . .

47

For the Lord your God is a devouring fire, a jealous God. . . . I call heaven and earth to witness against you this day that if you act corruptly you will soon utterly perish from the land which you are going over the Jordan to possess; you will not live long upon it, but will be utterly destroyed. And the Lord will scatter you among the peoples, and you will be left few in number among the nations where the Lord will drive you" (Dt. 4:23-27).

The truth of this and comparable warnings was demonstrated most graphically by the overthrow of both the temple and the city of Jerusalem in 587 B.C. by Nebuchadnezzar and the Babylonian captivity which resulted, and by the similar devastation inflicted by the hands of the Roman armies in A.D. 70.

Such catastrophic events could not have failed to call to mind the solemn words with which God had admonished Solomon, under whose supervision the original magnificent temple had been constructed:

"If you turn aside and forsake my statutes and my commandments which I have set before you, and go and serve other gods and worship them, then I will pluck you up from the land which I have given you; and this house, which I have consecrated for my name, I will cast out of my sight, and will make it a proverb and a byword among all peoples. And at this house, which is exalted, every one passing by will be astonished, and say, 'Why has the Lord done thus to this land and to this house?' Then they will say, 'Because they forsook the Lord the God of their fathers who brought them out of the land of Egypt, and laid hold on other gods, and worshipped them and served them; therefore he has brought all this evil upon them' " (2 Chron. 7:19-22).

Certainly, those Jews who returned to Jerusalem from the Babylonian captivity acknowledged the guilt of their nation and the justness of the punishment that had overtaken them:

"Thou hast been just in all that has come upon us, for

48

thou hast dealt faithfully and we have acted wickedly; our kings, our princes, our priests, and our fathers have not kept thy law or heeded thy commandments and thy warnings which thou didst give them. They did not serve thee in their kingdom, and in thy great goodness which thou gavest them, and in the large and rich land which thou didst set before them; and they did not turn from their wicked works. Behold, we are slaves this day; in the land that thou gavest to our fathers to enjoy its fruit and its good gifts, behold, we are slaves" (Neh. 9:33-36).

The rebellion and apostasy by which the people of Israel cut themselves off from the blessings of the covenant and brought disastrous judgment upon themselves did not nullify or invalidate God's covenant, however. The divine covenant was directed toward a definite goal, and nothing could frustrate the achievement of that goal. When Moses warned the Israelites of the dire consequences of unfaithfulness to God ("you will soon utterly perish from the land") he also held out the hope of restoration for those who, though dispersed among the nations, repented and turned to God for grace:

"But from there you will seek the Lord your God, and you will find him, if you search after him with all your heart and with all your soul. When you are in tribulation, and all these things come upon you in the latter days, you will return to the Lord your God and obey his voice, for the Lord your God is a merciful God; he will not fail you or destroy you or forget the covenant with your fathers which he swore to them" (Dt. 4:29-31).

Human sinfulness, though it leads to judgment instead of blessing, cannot undo what God has decreed. His purposes are everlasting and his covenant stands sure. The history of the Israelites, then, should be a solemn reminder that privilege involves responsibility, that to hear and to have the word of God is not enough; it must also be believed and obeyed. By hardness

49

of heart and a rebellious spirit the most privileged proved itself to be the most irresponsible of nations, from whose ungodly example the warning is drawn: "Take care, brethren, lest there be in any of you an evil, unbelieving heart, leading you to fall away from the living God" (Heb. 3:12). To spurn the covenant is to forfeit its blessings and to cut oneself off from the line of promise.

GOD'S REMNANT

God was not taken by surprise by the unfaithfulness of the Israelites. He has his own way of accomplishing his purpose; and in particular it is through the faithful remnant that he is accustomed to work. This is strikingly illustrated in the case of Noah, who himself was God's remnant in his day, since he alone of that whole evil generation that was swept away by the flood was found righteous before God (Gen. 6:8, 9; 7:1), and he alone, together with his family, was preserved through that ordeal. The preservation of that very small remnant was at the same time the preservation of the line that was leading to the appearance of the promised seed of the woman.

Paul takes up this theme in his letter to the Christians in Rome and quotes the startling utterance of the prophet Isaiah: "Though the number of the sons of Israel be as the sand of the sea, only a remnant of them will be saved; for the Lord will execute his sentence upon the earth with rigor and dispatch" (Rom. 9:27f.; Is. 10:22). And he cites the complaint of God communicated through that same prophet: "All day long I have held out my hands to a disobedient and contrary people" (Rom. 10:21; Is. 65:2). But this does not imply the rejection of his people or the failure of his covenant.

> Do you not know what the scripture says of Elijah [he asks his readers], how he pleads with God against Israel? "Lord, they have killed thy prophets, they have demolished thy altars, and I alone am left, and they seek my life." But what is God's reply to him? "I have kept for myself seven thousand men who have not bowed the knee to Baal." So too at the present time there is a remnant, chosen by grace (Rom. 11:2-5; 1 Kings 19:10, 18).

Those who are chosen by God in accordance with his grace constitute his remnant. These are not stragglers who happen to be left in a day of national apostasy: they are the ones God has chosen and kept for himself. God is in sovereign control of all that comes to pass. He carries forward his purposes of blessing by means of his elect few. Through everything his grand design is majestically moving on to fulfilment.

THE TRUE ISRAELITE

Over and over again the descendants of Abraham, though as numerous as the sand of the seashore, invited the judgment of God upon themselves because they were a rebellious and stiff-necked people, and it was only because of the faithful core or remnant among them that the nation was preserved from total destruction. "If the Lord of hosts had not left us a seed," said Isaiah, "we would have fared like Sodom and been made like Gomorrah" (Is. 1:9; Rom. 9:29). That is why Paul insists that "they are not all Israel who are of Israel, and not all are children of Abraham because

51

they are his seed" (Rom. 9:6f.). Mere external descent guarantees nothing. From the very beginning the remnant-principle is in operation: Cain, Eve's firstborn son, is externally the seed of the woman, but he shows himself to be in reality the seed of the serpent and not the seed of promise which he murders in the person of his younger brother Abel, and which, as we have seen, is restored in Seth.

Before the birth of Isaac, Abraham had a son Ishmael by the bondwoman Hagar; but when he besought the Lord, "O that Ishmael might live in thy sight!", that is, that he might be accepted as the son of the promise, God replied: "No, but Sarah your wife shall bear you a son, and you shall call his name Isaac. I will establish my covenant with him for his seed after him. . . . I will establish my covenant with Isaac" (Gen. 17:18-21). Accordingly, Isaac was chosen and not Ishmael; and Paul sees this distinction between Ishmael and Isaac as symbolical of the fundamental distinction between those who are "born according to the flesh" and those who are "born according to the Spirit." The latter, "like Isaac, are children of promise" (Gal. 4:28f.). "This means," he explains in his letter to the Romans, "that it is not the children of the flesh who are the children of God, but the children of the promise are reckoned as seed" (Rom. 9:8). Why should the Jew who boasts of his descent from Abraham and yet despises his privileges and wilfully breaks the law of God expect to meet with divine favor? To such a person Paul sternly says: "By your hard and impenitent heart you are storing up wrath for yourself on the day of wrath when God's righteous judgment will be revealed" (Rom. 2:5). At the same time, and no less seriously, the way in which he dishonors God and abuses his goodness brings about the disgrace of which the prophet complained: "The name of God is blasphemed among the Gentiles because of you" (Rom. 2:24; Is. 52:5).

Nor will it avail for him to plead that as a Jew he

has received the covenant sign of circumcision, for, again, the outward and visible sign when divorced from the inward and spiritual grace to which it points is a mark of condemnation rather than blessing. His conduct contradicts the sacrament, indeed puts it into reverse, so to speak. "If you break the law," Paul tells the Jew, "your circumcision becomes uncircumcision"; and this leads on to the important explanation:

> For he is not a real Jew who is one outwardly, nor is true circumcision something external and physical. He is a Jew who is one inwardly, and real circumcision is a matter of the heart, spiritual and not literal. His praise is not from men but from God (Rom. 2:25, 28f.).

This is no novel understanding of the meaning of the rite of circumcision, for this emphasis on its true inward significance is in fact founded on the plain teaching of the Old Testament. There was therefore no reason for the devout Jew to be in error concerning its real import, or to confide in it as though by itself circumcision guaranteed nationalistic superiority as well as immunity from divine displeasure. Thus in Leviticus 26:41 the nation, though fastidious in observing the external administration of circumcision, is rebuked because of its "uncircumcised heart"; and Moses, after stressing that what God required of them was "to fear the Lord your God, to walk in all his ways, to love him, to serve the Lord your God with all your heart and with all your soul," urges the Israelites to cease being stubborn and to be circumcised in their hearts (Dt. 10:12-16; cf. 30:6); and later on, at another time of national crisis, the prophet Jeremiah warned the inhabitants of Judah that if they were not circumcised in their hearts God's wrath would "go forth like fire, and burn with none to quench it, because of the evil of [their] doings" (Jer. 4:3f.; cf. 9:26).

The same principle of inward integrity as opposed

to mere outward formalism applies with equal validity to the Christian believer, who in Christ has been "circumcised with a circumcision made without hands, by putting off the body of flesh in the circumcision of Christ" — which in fact is the inner significance of baptism as it speaks to us of burial with Christ and death to the old life of sin, and resurrection with Christ to newness of life in the Spirit (Col. 2:11f.). That is why Paul is able to say that Christians are "the true circumcision, who worship by the Spirit of God, and glory in Christ Jesus, and put no confidence in the flesh" (Phil. 3:3). It is precisely in those "who walk not according to the flesh but according to the Spirit" that "the just requirement of the law" is fulfilled (Rom. 8:4).

A SEAL OF THE RIGHTEOUSNESS OF FAITH

Abraham was not justified by his own works but by faith in God's word, Paul argues, citing Genesis 15:6: "Abraham believed God, and it was reckoned to him as righteousness." It is by faith that the grace of God is appropriated. But now the important question for the Jew — and especially the self-righteous Pharisee, such as Paul himself had once been (Phil. 3:4-6) — was whether God's blessing is "pronounced only upon the circumcised, or also upon the uncircumcised"; and the answer is to be found in the history of Abraham, because his faith was reckoned as righteousness to him not after but **before** he was circumcised. The blessing came first; consequently his circumcision could in no sense be regarded as the gateway to blessing. Grace always comes first. The sacrament is added as a seal which confirms the truth of the promise that has been believed. The logic of all this is inescapable, as Paul explains:

> Abraham received the sign of circumcision as a seal of the righteousness which he had by faith while he was still uncircumcised. The purpose was to make him the father of all who believe without being circumcised and who thus have righteousness reckoned to them, and likewise the father of the circumcised who are not merely circumcised but also follow the example of the faith which our father Abraham had before he was circumcised (Rom. 4:11-12).

In the most profound sense, therefore, Abraham is the father, not of those who can trace their physical descent from him or of those who have received the external mark of circumcision, but of those who, like him, are justified by faith in the promise of God's grace. The blessing of the promise depends on faith

> in order that the promise may rest on grace and be guaranteed to all his seed—not only to the adherents of the law [i.e. Jews] but also to those who share the faith of Abraham [i.e. although they are not Jews], for he is the father of us all, as it is written, "I have made you the father of many nations" [not just of one nation] (Rom. 4:13-17; Gen. 17:5).

The argument recurs in the Epistle to the Galatians, where, on the basis of the same premise, namely, that "Abraham believed God and it was reckoned to him as righteousness," Paul draws the conclusion: "So you see that it is men of faith who are the sons of Abraham." Indeed, he asserts, using a striking figure of speech, that "the scripture foresaw that God would justify the Gentiles by faith" and actually "preached the gospel beforehand to Abraham" in the words of the promise, "In you shall all the nations be blessed" (Gen. 12:3). It is evident, then, that "those who are men of faith are blessed with Abraham who had faith" (Gal.

3:6-9). **Faith,** of course, does not mean faith in a vacuum or blind faith, which would be a contradiction in terms; for genuine faith must have an object, and in Holy Scripture the object of faith is the word of God, or, still more specifically, that Person who himself is the Word of God incarnate (Jn. 1:1, 14). "In Christ Jesus all [Gentiles as well as Jews] are sons of God, through faith," Paul affirms:

> For as many of you as were baptized into Christ have put on Christ. There is neither Jew nor Greek, there is neither slave nor free, there is neither male nor female; for you are all one in Christ Jesus. And if you are Christ's, then you are Abraham's seed, heirs according to promise (Gal. 3:26-29).

The teaching of Paul which we have been considering to this point may be summed up as follows: to be a **physical** descendant of Abraham is not an automatic passport to acceptance with God, as the history of the Israelites demonstrates; what is essential is to be a **spiritual** descendant of Abraham, that is, to be one who, like Abraham, through divine grace is justified by faith; in this deep sense Abraham, who himself was uncircumcised when God blessed and justified him, is the father of all who believe, no matter what their race or social status may be, and so he is the father not of one but of many nations; these children of Abraham, because they are born according to the Spirit, are indeed the sons of God, and from generation to generation they constitute the faithful remnant, chosen by grace.

The theology of this theme is most fully developed by Paul, but it is a theme which pervades the whole of of the New Testament and which has its roots in the terms themselves of the Abrahamic covenant with its promise of universal blessing. The New Testament authors were Jews who had come to faith in Christ and the whole purpose of whose lives was to propagate that faith throughout the world. John's Gospel, for example, was written that people might "believe that Jesus is the Christ, the Son of God, and that believing they might have life in his name" (Jn. 20:31). Believers in Christ are, as we have seen, the true seed of Abraham, the father of those who believe (Gal. 3:26-29; Rom. 4:11). John the Baptist was not in the least swayed by the consideration that those who flocked to hear his preaching in the wilderness were the children of Abraham "according to the flesh." When many of the Pharisees and Sadducees, the religious élite of Judaism, approached him for baptism he denounced them and their narrow nationalism in the most uncompromising manner, addressing them not as sons of Abraham but as a "brood of vipers"!

> "Who warned you to flee from the wrath to come? Bear fruit that befits repentance, and do not presume to say to yourselves, 'We have Abraham as our father'; for I tell you, God is able from these stones to raise up children to Abraham" (Mt. 3:7-9).

Surrounded by a hostile company of Jews who confidently announced, "We are Abraham's seed," Jesus (himself a descendant of Abraham) replied: "I know that you are Abraham's seed; yet you seek to kill me, because my word finds no place in you. I speak of what I have seen with my Father, and you do what you have heard from your father." Though both Jesus and his adversaries shared, as fellow Jews, the fatherhood of Abraham as their common ancestor, yet, with unmistakable significance, he makes a distinction between his father and theirs. They rejoin with the assertion, "Abraham is our father," which is in effect a repetition of the claim they have previously made. But then Jesus makes it absolutely plain that in the ultimate issue there are but two fatherhoods, one of God and the other of Satan:

> "If you were Abraham's children, you would do what

57

Abraham did, but now you seek to kill me, a man who
has told you the truth which I heard from God; this
is not what Abraham did. You do what your father did.
. . . If God were your Father, you would love me,
for I proceeded and came forth from God; I came not
of my own accord, but he sent me. Why do you not
understand what I say? It is because you cannot bear
to hear my word. *You are of your father the devil,*
and your will is to do your father's desires. He was
a murderer from the beginning, and has nothing to do
with the truth, because there is no truth in him" (Jn.
8:33-44).

Children of Abraham they might be by external descent, but in the inner reality of their being they were
children of the Devil. When hearts are faithless and
unregenerate the reception of rites and sacraments,
divinely given though they be, makes a mockery of the
grace of which they are intended to be signs and seals.
This consideration explains the vehement words of condemnation with which the first martyr Stephen assailed
the dignified members of the ecclesiastical court which
had assembled to pronounce condemnation on him for
his preaching of the Gospel of God's grace in Christ
Jesus: "You stiff-necked persons, uncircumcised in
heart and ears, you always resist the Holy Spirit"
(Acts 7:51).

THE SINGULAR SEED OF ABRAHAM

Sufficient evidence has been adduced to show that the
promise to Abraham of a numerous "seed" was suscep-
tible of two different interpretations, both of which
are present in Scripture. First, there was an outward
meaning in accordance with which Abraham's posterity became a great and populous nation. But, secondly,

the promise had an inner significance which finds its fulfilment in all who follow Abraham's example of genuine faith in God, all, that is to say, who, irrespective of whether they can claim fleshly descent from Abraham or not, are born of the Spirit. But there is a more profound sense still in which the promise of a "seed" to Abraham is seen as having been fulfilled, namely, that that "seed" achieves its realization **in the single person of Christ.** It is to Christ that the line of promise moves, and in Christ that it attains its goal and its fulness. Christ, and Christ alone, is the true "remnant." He alone is born of God. The theological implications of this truth are of the utmost importance.

The perception of Abraham's faith was so penetrating that, as we have remarked above, he was able to look beyond the transient territory of Canaan to the glorious reality of that eternal homeland which God has prepared for his people. By faith he laid hold of the perfection of the new heaven and the new earth in which all God's purposes of creation and grace will be brought to completion. But the focal point of his perspective was not the resplendent vista of eternal blessing but rather **the person** of him who is the Mediator of all blessing. It was the advent of Christ, the promised "seed" **par excellence**, for which he looked and longed. "Your father Abraham rejoiced that he was to see my day," Christ assured his unfriendly critics; and so real and substantial was the hope evinced by the promise that (Christ added) "he saw it and was glad" (Jn. 8:56).

In a similar manner Paul expounds the innermost significance of the covenant promises given to Abraham: "Now the promises were made to Abraham and to his seed. It does not say, 'And to seeds,' referring to many; but, referring to one, 'And to your seed,' which is Christ" (Gal. 3:16). The apostle does not overlook the fact that the noun "seed" can also be used as a collective noun to denote many persons rather than just

59

one; in fact he uses it in this sense in this very passage. But the point is that before God there is only one person who is properly the "seed" of Abraham. The incarnate Son is the sole son with whom God is well pleased (Mt. 3:17; 17:5). In him uniquely God's word spoken through his prophet is fulfilled: "Behold, my servant whom I have chosen, my beloved with whom my soul is well pleased" (Mt. 12:18; Is. 42:1). It follows that those many persons who collectively are the "seed" of Abraham can be so only on condition that they are made one with him who alone is the true "seed." Since "all have sinned and fall short of the glory of God" (Rom. 3:23), Jesus Christ, who alone is without sin and in whom alone God has been fully glorified (Heb. 4:15; 7:26f.; 1 Pet. 2:22; 3:18; 1 Jn. 3:5; Jn. 17:4), is the sole faithful "remnant."

Union with Christ is essential for all who wish to be truly the children of Abraham and to enjoy the blessings of the covenant. That is why the New Testament is so insistent that the believer's standing and acceptance before God is not at all in himself but only and altogether **in Christ.** Paul accordingly, in this same passage where he explains that Christ is uniquely the "seed" of Abraham, gives his readers this assurance: **"In Christ Jesus** you are **all sons of God,** through faith. . . . **You are all one in Christ Jesus.** And if you are Christ's, then **you are Abraham's seed,** heirs according to promise" (Gal. 3:26-29).

BLESSING FOR THE WORLD

The purpose of God's covenant with Abraham was one of blessing to the whole world. We have seen that the promises of that covenant were never intended to foster an exclusive spirit of national superiority on the part of those who were Abraham's descendants according to the flesh or to encourage the notion that the Gentile nations were beyond the scope of God's grace. That from the very beginning it was God's plan to "justify the Gentiles by faith" is plain from the covenant assurance repeatedly given to Abraham that in his seed all the nations of the earth would be blessed (Gal. 3:8; Gen. 12:3; 18:18; 22:18). God's choosing of Abraham and his posterity was designed to bring blessing to all; indeed, the evidence of this truth, far from being limited to the history of God's dealings with Abraham, is present in every section of the Old Testament. Consequently, there was no excuse for the temper of pharisaic exclusivisim which had become so prevalent in Palestine by the time of the incarnation.

Paul in the Epistle to the Romans (9:24-26; 10:11-13, 19-21) reminds his readers of those prophetic words of Hosea which strike at the root of nationalistic pride: "Those who were not my people I will call 'my people,' and her who was not beloved I will call 'my beloved' "; and again: "In the very place where it was said to them, 'You are not my people,' they will be called 'sons of the living God' " (Hos. 2:23; 1:10). The declaration of Isaiah that "no one who believes in him will be put to shame" (Is. 28:16) points to the fact that "there is no distinction between Jew and Greek" and that "the same Lord is Lord of all and bestows his riches upon all who call upon him," for, as another prophet proclaimed, "every one who calls upon the name of the Lord will be saved" (Joel 2:32). Paul recalls how Moses predicted, prior to the entry of the

Israelites into the promised land: "I will make you jealous of those who are not a nation; with a foolish nation I will make you angry" (Dt. 32:12); and how God had said through Isaiah: "I have been found by those who did not seek me; I have shown myself to those who did not ask for me"; whereas of Israel it was said: "All day long I have held out my hands to a disobedient and a contrary people" (Is. 65:1f.).

Later in the same epistle (Rom. 15:8-12) the apostle cites more passages from the writings of the Old Testament which show that the purpose of Christ's coming was "in order to confirm the promises given to the patriarchs and in order that the Gentiles might glorify God for his mercy": first from the book of Psalms: "I will praise thee among the Gentiles and sing to thy name" (Ps. 18:49); then from the Pentateuch: "Rejoice, O Gentiles, with his people" (Dt. 32:43); then from another psalm: "Praise the Lord, all nations, and let all the peoples praise him" (Ps. 117:1); and finally from the prophecy of Isaiah: "The root of Jesse shall come, he who rises to rule the Gentiles; in him shall the Gentiles hope" (Is. 11:10). The truth, however, to which the Jew persistently closed his mind was that "there is no respect of persons with God" (Rom. 2:11). He was unwilling to admit that the universal grace of God is founded upon the universal sinfulness of mankind, because this clearly meant that the Jew no less than the Gentile was in need of salvation. He found it more congenial to imagine that his acceptance with God followed from the precision of his religious observances coupled with his descent from Abraham and his allegiance to the promised land, the holy city of Jerusalem, and the temple of God, though the history of his nation loudly proclaimed the inadequacy of such connections.

STEPHEN'S SPEECH

God is not impressed with the sanctimony of religious punctilio, nor are his power and presence restricted to any earthly territory or city or temple. This in fact is the thrust of Stephen's address to the members of the Sanhedrin in Jerusalem (Acts 7), delivered with such piercing effectiveness that his hearers were cut to the heart. What they heard was not a simple recital of the past history of their people (as the casual reader might judge it to be), but a methodical presentation of facts whose factuality none could question and which were therefore all the more devastating as a means of demolishing the foundations of their self-righteous pretensions. To bring out this emphasis which pervades the speech we shall summarize it as follows:

"Our great forefather Abraham [Stephen says to them in effect], of whose stock you boast yourselves to be, was actually **a foreigner, a Chaldean** by birth. God manifested himself to him **in Mesopotamia,** not in Judea. Indeed, in the promised land the patriarch had not even a square foot of soil to call his own, with the exception of a place of **burial** which he had to purchase from the inhabitants for a sum of money. Even this sepulchre was located in a place despised by you — **Shechem,** a city of the Samaritans with whom you have no dealings. There was no city of Jerusalem and no temple in the land in his day. The ancestors you venerate wickedly sold their brother Joseph **into Egypt;** but **God was with him** in that foreign country. It was **in Egypt,** not Judea, that the insignificant handful of your forefathers had to take refuge in order that they might survive and not all perish from starvation. Again, it was **in Egypt** that the Israelites became a great and numerous people. Your famous leader and lawgiver Moses was born **in Egypt;** he was nurtured and educated **in the palace of Pharaoh,** and became learned in **Egyptian** wisdom. I remind you, too, that your forebears rejected Moses as their leader and deliverer when he wished to help them, and caused him to flee and become a sojourner in the strange land of **Midian** for a third part of his lifetime. Yet God appeared to him **in that wilderness**, and proclaimed the locality of his manifestation, though alien soil, to be **holy ground.** The law and oracles of God were communicated to Moses at **Mount Sinai** in **Arabia**, not in the promised land; and for forty years he led the Israelites **through the wilderness.** God showed his wonders and signs to them **in Egypt** and **at the Red Sea** and **in the wilderness**, heathen territory, all of it; yet your ancestors, whose memory you so proudly cherish, were disobedient, rebellious, idolatrous, and unmindful of all God's goodness to them. Even the divinely ordained tabernacle was a **wilderness** institution; and some hundreds of years later, in the days of the great king David, there was still no temple in the city of David, though he found favor with God and earnestly desired to build him a house. This privilege was granted to Solomon, the king who nonetheless was responsible for setting the nation off on the disastrous decline toward the idolatry and apostasy which ended in the shame of the Assyrian and Babylonian captivities. But the infinite Deity, the Most High, is not a man that he should need a house, however magnificent, as his dwelling. You, who boast with such self-confidence about your man-made temple, as though you had Almighty God for ever confined within it, have evidently forgotten the word of God spoken through the prophet Isaiah: 'Heaven is my throne, and earth my footstool. What house will you build for me, says the Lord, or what is the place of my rest?' (Is. 66:1f.). But what do you care about the teaching of the prophets, obstinate and unregenerate resisters of the Holy Spirit as you are? Were there any of the prophets whom your fathers did not persecute? And now, just as they killed those

64

who foretold the coming of the Righteous One, so you in turn have betrayed and put to death that Righteous One!"

A prophetic voice indeed! But these religious leaders immediately proved the justness of Stephen's words as, inflamed with rage, they dragged him outside the city and stoned him to death, thus adding another name to the long list of those who have been summarily silenced because they chose to speak God's truth rather than to purchase ease by the utterance of smooth deceits. As always, however, God had his replacement at hand, on this occasion another young man of outstanding ability, Saul of Tarsus, who by the miraculous power of God's grace would be transformed from the fierce persecutor of Christ's followers into the great apostle to the Gentiles, the evangelist with a message for the whole world (see Acts 7:58; 8:1-3; 9:1ff.). Paul himself would suffer, like Stephen, the intense antagonism of his fellow Jews. This caused him great anguish of heart, because by their narrow self-righteousness they not only cut themselves off from the long-promised blessing, now fulfilled by Christ's coming, which they should have been the first to welcome, but also prevented others from entering the kingdom of God (Mt. 23:13).

THE LAW OF MOSES

Stephen was accused, as also Paul would be after him, of conspiring to overthrow the temple in Jerusalem and subvert the law of Moses, the two institutions most sacred to Judaism (Acts 6:13f.; 21:28). Both protested their innocence of any such intention — Stephen by implication throughout his "defense," which was based on the books of Moses, and Paul quite explicitly (Acts 25:8; 28:17). The charge was in fact essentially the same as had been brought against Jesus at his trial (Mk. 14:58; Lk. 23:5, 14). But Jesus was certainly not hostile to Moses. If there was unfaithfulness to the doctrine of Moses, it was not he but his critics who, despite their boast that they were Moses' disciples (Jn. 9:28f.; Rom. 2:17ff.), were guilty of such unfaithfulness. "If you believed Moses, you would believe me," he told them. "But if you do not believe his writings, how will you believe my words?" (Jn. 5:46f.). He gently chided Cleopas and his friend on the road to Emmaus for being "slow to believe all that the prophets had written," and then, to demonstrate the necessity that "the Christ should suffer these things and enter into his glory," from "Moses and all the prophets he interpreted to them in all the scriptures the things concerning himself." And again, shortly afterward, he explained to the apostles the reason for his death and resurrection: "These are my words which I spoke to you while I was still with you," he said, "that everything written about me in the law of Moses and the prophets and the psalms must be fulfilled"; and "he opened their minds to understand the scriptures" (Lk. 24:25-27, 44f.). In short, as he assured his listeners in the course of his sermon on the mount, Jesus did not come to abolish the law and the prophets but to fulfil them (Mt. 5:17).

In speaking of the law of Moses our concern here is not with the multiplicity of regulations relating to ritual, culture, hygiene, and the daily administration of civic affairs, but with the **moral** law which was the true heart of the Mosaic legislation. This moral law is summed up in the code universally known as the Ten Commandments, and the essence of the Ten Commandments is given in the response of Jesus to the scribe who asked him, "Which commandment is the first of all?", to which he answered:

> You shall love the Lord your God with all your heart,
> and with all your soul, and with all your mind. This
> is the great and first commandment. And the second is
> like it, You shall love your neighbor as yourself. On
> these two commandments depend all the law and the
> prophets (Mt. 22:35-40; Dt. 6:5; Lev. 19:18).

In a single word, **love** is what the law is all about. And
this is precisely what Paul affirms when he says that
"love is the fulfilling of the law" (Rom. 13:10). Failure
to keep the law is a failure of love.

Contrary, then, to those voices which tell us that
the law and love are fundamentally opposed to each
other, the former being rigid and harsh and insensitive
and the latter, by contrast, gentle and flexible and con-
siderate, the biblical teaching insists that the law and
love belong together, that the latter is the expression
of the former. To those who wish to find fault with
the law Paul rejoins that it is in fact "holy" and "just"
and "good" and "spiritual" (Rom. 7:12, 14); and it
is so simply because it is **God's** law: what comes from
God cannot be faulted. The law was given to Moses in
the presence of God's glory, with the result that "the
Israelites could not look on Moses' face because of its
brightness" (2 Cor. 3:7). The objection that the apostle
seems to see the law in a less favorable light when he
describes it as "the dispensation of condemnation" and
"the dispensation of death" carries no weight because
he does so in the very passage where he insists on the
gloriousness of the law's origin (2 Cor. 3:7, 9). It is
not the law that is at fault but man because he is a
law-breaker. This is the whole point of the seventh
chapter of Romans.

In itself, indeed, the law is a principle of life, not
of death. It prescribes the divine standard, which is
the standard of total love. This, obviously, is the way
of life, because it is the way of harmony, joy, and fulfilment, in our relation both to the Creator, the source
of all life, and to the creation of which we are part.

67

Thus God said to Moses that it was by keeping his statutes and ordinances that "a man shall live" (Lev. 18:5; see also Neh. 9:29; Ezek. 20:11, 13, 21); and this is also the understanding of Paul (Rom. 10:5). Paul, however, because like all other men he was a breaker of God's law, discovered that "the very commandment which promised life proved to be death to me" (Rom. 7:10). But death is not good; indeed, it is the negation of all that is good. "Did that which is good [the law], then, bring death to me?", he asks; and he immediately gives the emphatic reply:

> By no means! It was sin, working death in me through what is good, in order that sin might be shown to be sin, and through the commandment might become sinful beyond measure. We know that the law is spiritual: but I am carnal, sold under sin (Rom. 7:13f.).

As, however, the brilliance of the sun surpasses that of the moon, so the glory of the Gospel which brings justification instead of condemnation, and life in place of death, outshines the glory of the law (2 Cor. 3:7-11; 4:6).

THE MOSAIC COVENANT

The most prominent feature of the Mosaic dispensation, which continued in effect for many centuries until the advent of Christ, was the communication of the law of God to the Israelites and their commitment to the terms of God's covenant as specified in the demands of the Ten Commandments (Ex. 34:27ff.). This covenant mediated through Moses was not, however, an interruption of the covenant that God had made with

Abraham. Quite the contrary, for God's deliverance of the people from the bondage of Egypt under the leadership of Moses was in the closest possible connection with the covenant already established with Abraham (see, for example, Ex. 2:24). Thus Paul instructs the Galatian Christians that "the law, which came four hundred and thirty years afterward, does not annul a covenant previously ratified by God, so as to make the promise void" (Gal. 3:17). The covenant of grace, whereby the ungodly man is justified by faith, continues therefore without cessation or invalidation throughout the whole period of the dispensation of law under the Mosaic covenant. The latter covenant did not materially alter the situation. The law of Moses did not make man any more sinful or any less sinful; it neither diminished nor increased his need of divine grace.

What purpose, then, did the introduction of the Mosaic covenant serve? The answer to this question has already been indicated in Romans 7:13 quoted above. The law served to throw into relief the extreme sinfulness of sin: "in order that sin might be shown to be sin, and through the commandment might become sinful beyond measure." For if the keeping of the law is life, the breaking of the law is death (Rom. 6:23); and all men stand before God as law-breakers. But the law also served another purpose: by emphasizing the sinfulness of mankind it at the same time emphasized the need of mankind for the promised grace of God. Far from being contrary to the promises of God, the law, which shuts us all up together as sinners, makes plain the futility of trusting in any imagined righteousness of our own, and arouses in us the desire for the blessing promised to those who put their trust only in the word of God's grace. "The scripture consigned all things to sin," writes Paul, "that what was promised to faith in Jesus Christ might be given to those who believe." Consequently, he explains further, "the law was our attendant" — like the attendant who leads a child by the hand — "until Christ came, that we might be justified by faith. But now that faith has come, we are no longer under this attendant; for in Christ you are all sons of God through faith" (Gal. 3:21-26).

We see, therefore, that in an unexpected way the law is designed to help forward the blessing promised to Abraham. Turning us away from self-righteousness, or, as the older writers used to call it, works-righteousness, it encourages us to put our trust in someone other than ourselves, that One who alone, because he is the only law-keeper, is accepted by God, and who, by virtue of his offering of himself to death in our place, has made available to us the perfect life of his righteousness, Jesus Christ our Redeemer. By faith in him we too are assured of acceptance by God. Paul puts it in the following way:

> So then, those who are men of faith are blessed with Abraham who had faith. For all who rely on the works of the law are under a curse; for it is written, "Cursed be every one who does not abide by all things written in the book of the law, and do them" [Dt. 27:26]. Now it is evident that no man is justified before God by the law; for "He who through faith is righteous shall live" [Hab. 2:4]; but the law does not rest on faith, for "He who does them shall live by them." Christ redeemed us from the curse of the law, having become a curse for us — for it is written, "Cursed be every one who hangs on a tree" [Dt. 21:23] — that in Christ Jesus the blessing of Abraham might come upon the Gentiles, that we might receive the promise of the Spirit through faith (Gal. 3:9-14).

In this way it becomes evident that the law of Moses is, in the historic purpose of God, the coadjutor of the covenant made with Abraham, showing us as it does the emptiness of all self-righteousness and the absolute necessity of justification by faith in Christ

Jesus through whom the grace of God is freely made available to us. As from the very beginning of human history, and as with Abraham, so also throughout the centuries of the Mosaic dispensation, and equally in this final age in which we are living, the grace of God is the source of all blessing through Jesus Christ, in whom all the promises are confirmed and fulfilled (2 Cor. 1:20). "Therefore," the apostle declares,

> since we are justified by faith, we have peace with God through our Lord Jesus Christ. Through him we have obtained access to this grace in which we stand, and we rejoice in our hope of sharing the glory of God (Rom. 5:1-3).

THE AARONIC PRIESTHOOD

In the Old Testament the regulations governing the priesthood and the worship of the tabernacle (and later the temple) were an integral part of the Mosaic legislation. The law and the priesthood, in fact, were two aspects of the one system (cf. Heb. 7:11f.); and this was only to be expected in a community which regarded itself as a theocracy. Since the members of that community were sinful men and women, who constantly failed to meet the demands of the Ten Commandments to love God with the totality of their being and their fellow men as themselves, provisions were necessary not only for the civic government of society but also for the establishment of reconciliation between sinners and the God whose law they had violated. With this latter purpose in view, the tribe of Levi was set apart as the priestly tribe and, within that tribe, Aaron and his sons were designated to serve as high priests. Their duties included the daily service of the tabernacle and the offering of sacrifices in expiation of the sins of the people.

The levitical system, however, was an interim system, for the reason that it was incompetent to deal with human sinfulness in depth. The law could not meet the need for radical transformation because, as law, it can justify only the person who completely fulfils what it commands: the law-breaker it can but condemn (cf. Jas. 2:10). That is why, as we have seen, the sinner must look elsewhere for justification. The inability of the Aaronic priesthood to achieve what was portended by its sacrificial system is apparent from the following considerations.

(1) The imperfection of the Aaronic priesthood is evident in that in this order there was a multiplicity of priests; and this was because these priests (and high priests) were **mortal** men who in turn were carried away by death, so that there was a long succession of priests from one generation to another. A perfect priesthood required the appearance of a single person whose life and priesthood continued forever, without interruption by death.

(2) But as well as being mortal the levitical priests were **sinful** men (and of course sin and death are closely associated in Scripture: "death came into the world through sin," Rom. 5:12). This fact in itself is sufficient to account for the inadequacy of their priesthood. Consequently, before offering a sacrifice for the sins of the people they had to offer up a sacrifice for their own sins.

(3) Not only was there a multiplicity of priests, but there was also a multiplicity of sacrifices. Over and over again, day after day, year after year, sacrifices for sin were offered — a fact which gave eloquent witness to the inadequacy of the levitical sacrifices; for the perfect sacrifice must be one which avails once and for all and which by reason of the completeness of its efficacy brooks no repetition.

(4) The principle in accordance with which these sacrifices operated was that of **substitution**. This is illustrated with great clarity in the ritual of the day of atonement, which in so many respects was the climax of the levitical year. On that great annual occasion the high priest offered a bull as a sin offering for himself. He then took two goats and killed one of them as a sin offering for the people. The blood of sacrifice was carried by the high priest into the tabernacle, through the outer chamber known as the holy place and into the inner sanctuary or the holy of holies, where it was sprinkled on the mercy-seat to make atonement for the sins of all. The high priest alone was permitted to enter the holy of holies and then only once a year on the day of atonement. On coming out again from the tabernacle he took the other goat, laid his hands on its head, and over it confessed the sins of the people of Israel, and it was then led away into the wilderness where it was released, never to be seen again (Lev. 16). In this way the provision of atonement through the death of another as a substitute for the sinner, and the effective removal of his sins, was graphically symbolized. But the inability of this ceremony to achieve what it symbolized is apparent from the fact that it had to be repeated every year — not to mention the various other sin-offerings which were presented from day to day. Moreover, a brute beast is no proper substitute for God's creature man who is made in the image of his Creator. An animal without reason, without comprehension, without a will or a conscience of its own, can never take the place of the sinner, who is a sinner precisely because he is a person possessing awareness and volition and rationality and a sense of right and wrong, and therefore one who is answerable to his Maker. Only one who is truly man and without sin would be qualified to do this.

It would be a mistake to conclude, however, that the levitical system was without value or meaning, or

73

that the Israelites had no experience of the pardoning grace of God. From the very beginning, as we have shown, God is the God of grace, and throughout the period of the law the Abrahamic covenant with its principle of faith and blessing continued in force. The Aaronic priesthood and its sacrifices were anticipatory and preparatory. They were not an end in themselves, but they pointed forward to the reality of that priesthood and that sacrifice which would be perfect and forever effective. In other words, they were genuinely **sacramental.** In dramatic manner these ceremonies spoke of the way of atonement as one which involved the death of a spotless victim as the sinner's substitute, and of the need for a high priest who would enter on their behalf into the sanctuary of God's presence not just once a year but once for all, and who at the same time would open the way for all into that same glory from which, as the barrier of the curtain in the tabernacle symbolized, their sins excluded them.

THE ORDER OF MELCHIZEDEK

The Old Testament does in fact mention an order of priesthood other than that of Aaron, for in Psalm 110:4 we read: "The Lord has sworn and will not change his mind, 'You are a priest for ever after the order of Melchizedek.' " This brief declaration is remarkable because it speaks of a priest who, unlike the levitical priests, is a priest **forever**, and also because of its mention of Melchizedek. What little we know about Melchizedek comes from a short passage in the book of Genesis (the only other place in the Old Testament where he is mentioned) which describes how, when

Abraham returned after defeating the eastern kings who had carried off his nephew Lot, Melchizedek, "king of Salem" and "priest of God Most High," met him and provided bread and wine for his refreshment. We are told, further, that Melchizedek blessed Abraham and that Abraham gave Melchizedek a tenth part of the spoils he had taken (Gen. 14:17-20). In the New Testament the name of Melchizedek occurs only in the Epistle to the Hebrews, whose author explains the significance of this encounter with Abraham and of the statement in Psalm 110. He draws attention to the typical correspondences between Melchizedek and Christ, the incarnate Son of God. The appropriateness of the name "Melchizedek," which means "king of righteousness," and the office, "king of Salem," which means "king of peace," and, simultaneously, "priest of the Most High God," is obvious, for in Christ, who is "the Lord our righteousness" (Jer. 23:6; 33:16) and the "Prince of peace" (Is. 9:6), the kingly and priestly offices are perfectly combined. Indeed, the very silence of Scripture is seen as significant, because, contrary to custom, in the case of Melchizedek no genealogy is given; there is no mention of parentage or of posterity. In this, too, he "resembles the Son of God" who "continues a priest for ever." Furthermore, that Melchizedek received tithes from Abraham and gave him his blessing designates him as superior to Abraham, for tithes are paid by the lesser to the greater person, and blessing is conveyed from the greater to the lesser. This, in effect, suggests the superiority of Melchizedek not only to Abraham but also to Levi who, at the time when Abraham was paying homage to Melchizedek, was, so to speak, "in the loins" of his ancestor, and so did homage together with him. This indicates the superiority of the priesthood of Melchizedek to that of Levi (or Aaron).

So much for the Genesis narrative; but the mention by the psalmist of "a priest for ever after the order of Melchizedek" is also full of meaning, because at the time when he wrote this the only priestly order was that of Levi — indeed, it was written in the mid-course of the Mosaic/Aaronic dispensation. If perfection had been attainable through the levitical priest-hood then prevailing, to speak of another order of priesthood would have been without point or purpose. To abolish and replace what is perfect would be sense-less. Therefore the very mention of another order implies the imperfection of the existing order.

It has been observed above that under the Mosaic/Aaronic system the law and the priesthood were in the closest association with each other. Accordingly, a change in the priesthood presupposes a change in the law. The law of Moses required that the priests of Israel should belong to the tribe of Levi, but with a change in the order of priesthood there comes also a change in this law; for the "priest for ever after the order of Melchizedek" of whom the psalmist spoke is Jesus Christ, the incarnate Son of God, and his human lineage is of the tribe of Judah, not Levi. In his case, moreover, the law of priestly succession is set aside, because he is a priest **forever**; his is "the power of an indestructible life," and his priesthood is both inde-fectible and intransmissible. His is a **unique** priesthood, fulfilled and concentrated in a single person. In con-trast to the former priests, he continues forever, and he is "holy, blameless, unstained, separated from sin-ners." Consequently, "he has no need, like those high priests, to offer sacrifices daily, first for his own sins and then for those of the people." This latter "he did once for all when he offered up himself" (Heb. 7).

He offered up **himself**! That is to say, he was both priest and victim, both offerer and offering. The sacri-fice of his priesthood was not that of bulls or goats, but of himself, our fellow human being. In him, at last, we have a true substitute, who genuinely and ade-quately took our place and died our death on the cross of Calvary; and this he did "once for all, the righteous for the unrighteous, that he might bring us to God" (1 Pet. 3:18). He has offered but one sacrifice, "once for all," because it is the perfect and all-sufficient sacrifice for the sins of the world. The constant repetition of the levitical sacrifices argues their imperfection. Had they been able to make the worshippers perfect they would have ceased to be offered. By their repetition they were a continual reminder of sin; "for it is impossible that the blood of bulls and goats should take away sins" (Heb. 10:1-4). How striking, then, is the contrast between this system and the order of Melchizedek; for, as the writer of the Epistle to the Hebrews says:

> When Christ had offered for all time a single sacrifice for sins, he sat down at the right hand of God, then to wait until his enemies should be made a stool for his feet. For by a single offering he has perfected for all time those who are sanctified (Heb. 10:12-14).

THE TRUE SANCTUARY

As the levitical high priest, on the day of atonement, used to slay the sacrificial victim on the altar of sacrifice in the courtyard of the tabernacle, and then would pass from the sight of the people into the inner sanctuary of the holy of holies, there to sprinkle the blood of atonement on the mercy-seat on their behalf, so Christ our great High Priest of the order of Melchizedek, when he had offered himself up on the altar of the cross, passed from our sight as the risen Lord into the heavenly sanctuary of God's presence. There, "seated at the right hand of the throne of the Majesty in heaven," he is "a minister in the sanctuary and the true tabernacle, which is set up not by man but by the Lord." The earthly sanctuary of the tabernacle (and the temple) was in fact "a copy and shadow of the heavenly sanctuary," which is the true and eternal sanctuary, "the greater and more perfect tabernacle" (Heb. 8:1-5; 9:11f.). And, as always, the coming of the reality and the substance means the disappearance of the copy and the shadow.

This, too, is the significance of the announcement of a new covenant; for the new supersedes the old, and it follows that "if that first [Mosaic] covenant had been faultless, there would have been no occasion for a second" (Heb. 8:7). But this is the undeniable implication of the announcement by the prophet Jeremiah of a new covenant at a time when the Mosaic covenant was in operation. He arouses the expectation of a better covenant when he proclaims:

> *"The days will come, says the Lord,*
> *when I will establish a new covenant with the house*
>   *of Israel*
> *and with the house of Judah;*
> *not like the covenant that I made with their fathers*
> *on the day when I took them by the hand*
> *to lead them out of the land of Egypt."*
>   (Heb. 8:8ff.; cf. Jer. 31:31f.)

Accordingly, the writer of the Epistle to the Hebrews presses home this conclusion: "In speaking of a new covenant he treats the former as obsolete. And what is becoming obsolete and growing old is ready to vanish away" (Heb. 8:13). This certainly must have been the perspective of Jeremiah when he prophesied that God would establish a new covenant with his people. It is important to notice that the contrast intended is between the new covenant and the former covenant which had been made through Moses, as the words of the prophecy clearly show. The reference is not in any way

78

to the abrogation or supersession of the covenant established with Abraham.

The passing of the Mosaic covenant involves also the passing of the levitical sanctuary and priesthood. The advent and the ascension of Christ have brought into being a new and wonderful relationship between earth and heaven; for the earth, on which the altar of the cross where the incarnate Son shed his atoning blood was raised, is now the forecourt of the true or heavenly sanctuary which our High Priest has entered on our behalf. He has disappeared from our sight into that true holy of holies; but all whose trust is in his blood-shedding look forward to his reappearance at the end of this age, having this assurance, that "Christ who was offered once to bear the sins of many will appear a second time, not to deal with sin but to save those who are eagerly waiting for him" (Heb. 9:28).

Meanwhile, however, there is no longer any curtain to exclude us from access into the holy presence of God. This was made plain in dramatic fashion at the moment of Christ's death on the cross when "the curtain of the temple was torn in two, from top to bottom" (Mt. 27:51; Mk. 15:38) — the detail "from top to bottom" indicating that this was the action of God, not man. No longer is it the high priest alone who is permitted to enter into that holiest sanctuary of God's presence, and that but once a year, while the people are denied this privilege; for in Christ God has reconciled the world to himself (2 Cor. 5:19), and thanks to the grace of this reconciliation the way is now open for all. Thus we are encouraged to "draw near with confidence to the throne of grace" (Heb. 4:16). Through the mediation of our High Priest of the order of Melchizedek we who are in the forecourt of this earth enjoy, even now, the privilege of unimpeded access to that inner shrine, "where Jesus has gone as a forerunner on our behalf" (Heb. 6:19f.).

79

THE NEW TEMPLE

The temple which Solomon built in Jerusalem was a structure of great magnificence, but it was destroyed in the early part of the sixth century B.C. during the sacking of the city by the Babylonian army. A new edifice was raised by those Jews who returned from exile under the leadership of Nehemiah some fifty years later; but it was only with the ambitious reconstruction carried out by Herod the Great, beginning in the year 19 B.C., that the former splendor was effectively restored. The work initiated by Herod continued, in fact, until A.D. 63, just a few years before temple and city were again devastated, this time by the soldiers of Caesar. This catastrophe was foreseen by Christ, who, when one of his disciples with understandable pride drew his attention to the architectural glories of the temple — "Look, Teacher, what wonderful stones and what wonderful buildings!" — , responded: "Do you see these great buildings? There will not be left here one stone upon another, that will not be thrown down" (Mk. 13:1f.). This act of destruction would be more than a misfortune of history, however, for it would mark the end of the era in which the worship of God had for its center an earthly temple. This was the significance of the assurance given by Jesus to the woman by the well at Sychar in Samaria: "Believe me, the hour is coming when neither on this mountain [Gerizim] nor in Jerusalem will you worship the Father" (Jn. 4:21).

With the accomplishment by Christ of his redemptive mission and the universal outpouring of the Holy Spirit, whose work is to apply the benefits of that redemption to the hearts of believers, the temple of God ceased to be a construction of stones and mortar. It is now **living** and **personal**. The place where God dwells and manifests his glory is now in the hearts and lives of his people. "Do you not know," Paul admonishes the Christians in Corinth, "that your body is a temple of the Holy Spirit within you, whom you have from God? You are not your own; you were bought with a price. So glorify God in your body" (I Cor. 6:19f.; cf. 3:16). Every believer, then, is God's temple. The redeemed heart is the inner shrine of the divine presence. The tablets of stone on which the Ten Commandments were written, and which were placed in the ark of the covenant within the holy of holies (I Kings 8:9; 2 Chr. 5:10; Heb. 9:4), have long since been lost. But the Ten Commandments have not been lost, and they are now, in accordance with the terms of the new covenant, located within that holy of holies which is the believing heart, inscribed there by the hand of God, who promised: "This is the covenant that I will make with the house of Israel after those days, says the Lord: I will put my laws into their minds, and write them upon their hearts" (Jer. 31:33; Heb. 8:10; cf. 2 Cor. 3:3, 6). To the same effect is the promise of Jesus himself: "If a man loves me, he will keep my word, and my Father will love him, and we will come to him and make our home with him" (Jn. 14:23).

Yet while it is possible to speak of separate Christians as temples in this manner, it would be a mistake to conclude that the overall picture is one of individualism. Rightly understood, he alone is God's true temple who has unfailingly kept God's law and honored his name, and, as we have seen, there is only one who has done this, namely, the incarnate Son. He alone could say to the Father with absolute truthfulness: "I glorified thee on the earth, having accomplished the work which thou hast given me to do" (Jn. 17:4). Of him alone could it be said that "he dwelt among us, full of grace and truth" (Jn. 1:14). In his life alone has the will of God been sanctified and enshrined (cf. Jn. 4:34). It is true of him alone that "in him the whole fulness of deity dwells bodily" (Col. 2:9). The supersession of the old temple by him who is the new temple is implied in his cryptic assertion: "Destroy this temple, and in three days I will raise it up." That he was not predicting any kind of miraculous rebuilding of a material temple in Jerusalem (which was the misunderstanding of his Jewish hearers) is made plain by John's explanatory comment: "He spoke of the temple of his body. When therefore he was raised from the dead, his disciples remembered that he had said this; and they believed the scripture and the word which Jesus had spoken" (Jn. 2:19-22).

The recognition of this truth leads to the conclusion that it is only through union with Christ, who himself is the true temple of God, that believers both individually and corporately can be spoken of as temples or as the temple of God. Thus Peter speaks of Christians as "living stones" who are "built into a spiritual house, to be a holy priesthood, to offer spiritual sacrifices to God through Jesus Christ" (1 Pet. 2:5); and Paul reassures the Gentile believers in Ephesus with these words:

> So then you are no longer strangers and sojourners, but you are fellow citizens with the saints and members of the household of God, built upon the foundation of the apostles and prophets, Christ Jesus himself being the cornerstone, in whom the whole structure is joined together and grows into *a holy temple in the Lord,* in whom you also are built into it for *a dwelling place of God in the Spirit* (Eph. 2:19-22).

Christ as the cornerstone gives alignment to the whole structure, which is being built up "to the measure of the stature of the fulness of Christ" (Eph. 4:13).

In harmony with this teaching is the description by John of his vision of the heavenly Jerusalem: "I saw no temple in the city," he says, "for its temple is the Lord God the Almighty, even the Lamb" — the Lamb being the designation of the eternal Son who by his assumption of our humanity and his sacrifice of himself on the cross (the Lamb of God taking away the sin of the world, Jn. 1:29) has redeemed our humanity, and who by his resurrection, ascension, and glorification has glorified our humanity. In this vision that holy temple which is now being built up in him is seen as having achieved its eternal completeness and perfection in the glory of him who is the Light of the world (Rev. 21:22f.; Jn. 8:12).

IS THERE A FUTURE FOR THE JEW?

We have seen that the New Testament clearly teaches that God's promise to Abraham of blessing to all the nations of the world through his seed is fulfilled in the single person and the unique work of Jesus Christ; that those only are the true children of Abraham who are united by faith to him who is the singular seed; that the union of believers in Christ means the end of the age-old distinction between Jew and Gentile, that the new wine of the Gospel cannot be contained in the old wineskin of the Mosaic system, with the result that the old order of Aaron has been superseded by the new order of Melchizedek, of which Christ is the sole, ever living high priest, and the levitical sacrifices by the one, all-availing sacrifice of himself offered by the incarnate Son in our stead; and that the earthly temple has been replaced by a new and living spiritual temple in which God and his glory dwell forever. Do these important considerations mean that since the coming of Christ there is no longer any justification for differentiating between Jew and Gentile?

The answer to this question is **Yes** for those who as fellow believers are one in Christ, and for whom consequently this distinction has completely fallen away. But in the sphere of missionary or evangelistic endeavor the answer is **No;** that is to say, in the presentation of the Gospel the difference between Jew and Gentile still has meaning. This does not at all imply, however, that there is one gospel for the Jew and another for the Gentile. "The same Lord is the Lord of all and bestows his riches upon all who call upon him," whether Jew or Gentile (Rom. 10:12). There is only one Mediator between God and men (1 Tim. 2:5), only one way back to the Father (Jn. 14:6), only one name given among men (whoever they may be) by which we must be saved (Acts 4:12). It was precisely one and the same Gospel which the apostles preached to both Jew and Gentile. Hence Paul's warning to the members of the Galatian church that anyone preaching a gospel other than that which they had heard and received through him was to be held as accursed (Gal. 1:6-9). Yet this same apostle, who so emphatically affirms the falling away of the differentiation between Jew and Gentile for those who are united in Christ, insists on retaining the differentiation in other respects.

This is not a simple differentiation, for there were ethnic diversities between Gentile and Gentile as well as between Jew and Gentile: the very term "Gentiles" designates the many nations in distinction from the single nation of the Jews. The differentiation is not a phenomenon at the level of merely human characteristics, but derives its profound significance from the fact that it rests on God's act in choosing Israel from among all the nations. "You are a people holy to the Lord your God," Moses told the Israelites:

> "The Lord your God has chosen you to be a people for his own possession, out of all the peoples that are on the face of the earth. It was not because you were more in number than any other people that the Lord set his love upon you and chose you, for you were the

84

fewest of all peoples; but it was because the Lord loves you, and is keeping the oath which he swore to your fathers, that the Lord has brought you out with a mighty hand, and redeemed you from the house of bondage" (Dt. 7:6-8).

God's choice of the Israelites was no **carte blanche**, however, permitting them to live carelessly without fear of retribution. Privilege always means responsibility. Hence the frequent warnings to them of the inevitability of judgment if they should turn aside from the loving service of their God. The following admonition is typical of many which they received from Moses:

> "If you are not careful to do all the words of this law which are written in this book, that you may fear this glorious and awful name, the Lord your God, then the Lord will bring on you and your offspring extraordinary afflictions, afflictions severe and lasting, . . . until you are destroyed. Whereas you were as the stars of heaven for multitude, you shall be left few in number; because you did not obey the voice of the Lord your God" (Dt. 28:58-62).

That these were not empty warnings is attested by the tragic history of the people of Israel, as over and over again their ingratitude and unfaithfulness brought on them the consequence of dire calamity.

Nor was the nation of Israel chosen because of any inherent goodness of its own. Far from it; for, as Paul clearly demonstrates in his Epistle to the Romans, "all men, both Jews and Greeks, are under the power of sin"; so that in respect of being sinners "there is no distinction, since all have sinned and fall short of the glory of God," and all, accordingly, whether Jews or Gentiles, are deserving of divine judgment and in need of divine grace (Rom. 3:9ff., 22f.). It was for purposes of blessing that the children of Israel were chosen by God — not blessing limited to themselves, however, but blessing intended for all the nations of the earth.

The blessing of the Jews is closely bound up with the blessing of the Gentiles. This consideration is of the greatest importance for a correct understanding of the place of the Jews in the purposes of God.

Of course, as we have previously explained, the blessing promised in and through the seed of Abraham has its particular fulfilment and concentration-point in the mediatorial person and work of Jesus Christ, who within the divine plan of redemption is the seed of Abraham in a unique sense. This in itself is blessing enough, to the Jews themselves, and to the world through the Jews! But at the same time the people of Israel were chosen and blessed in order that they might be a blessing to the world in a more general sense, though always within the sphere of the Gospel and its proclamation.

ISRAEL AND THE NATIONS

Jesus Christ, the promised Saviour, was "a light to lighten the Gentiles" as well as "the glory of [God's] people Israel" (Lk. 2:32). The latter were God's people because God had chosen them and enlightened them with his truth. They were specially blessed and privileged because, as Paul says, they were "entrusted with the oracles of God," and "to them belong the sonship, the glory, the covenants, the giving of the law, the worship, the promises, the patriarchs, and of their race, according to the flesh, is the Messiah" (Rom. 3:2; 9:4f.). It is true that prior to the coming of Christ the Israelites were a people apart, "a people holy to the Lord" (Dt. 7:6), who were strictly enjoined to avoid any sort of compromise with the ignorance and degradation of the nations by which they were surrounded (cf., for example, Dt. ch. 7; 29:16ff.) — though always there is the requirement that they should be just and hospitable to "the strangers within their gates" (cf. Ex. 22:21; 23:9; Dt. 1:16f.; 10:18f.). Indeed, the remarkable fact that women who were Gentile strangers (Rahab, Ruth) were actually brought into the line of promise that led to the birth of Christ (Mt. 1:5) is a further indication that in the purposes of God there was always a place for the participation of the nations in the blessing of which Israel was the vehicle.

But with the advent of Christ and the inauguration of the Gospel age there comes a striking change in the relationship between Israel and the nations. Now that the ancient promises have received their fulfilment in Christ (cf. 2 Cor. 1:20), Israel is no longer to hold herself aloof but is to carry the Good News to all the nations; for the glorious day that has now dawned upon us from on high brings not only "knowledge of salvation to God's people" but also "light to those who sit in darkness and in the shadow of death" (Lk. 1:77-79). Now the time has arrived for the blessing of all nations through the seed of Abraham, the time for all the nations to come and bow down before the Lord and to glorify his name (Ps. 86:9), the time for Israel to perform what the prophet Isaiah foresaw when he declared: "Behold, you shall call nations that you know not, and nations that knew you not shall run to you, because of the Lord your God and of the Holy One of Israel" (Is. 55:5).

This perspective displays the logic which justified the preaching of the Gospel first to the Jew and then to the Gentile. Of all the nations the Jewish people were in a special manner equipped to receive the Gospel, which was precisely the fulfilment of the divine promises and institutions which had been entrusted to them. They, before all others, should have recognized and welcomed Jesus as their Messiah — as did

Simeon and Anna who, looking on the child Jesus, perceived him to be the long-awaited Redeemer (Lk. 1:25-32, 36-38). And by the same token the Jews were in a special manner qualified to proclaim the Good News to the rest of the world. With this in mind, we can understand why Christ's brief earthly ministry was to all intents and purposes limited to the inhabitants of Palestine, and why Paul, though he was the apostle to the Gentiles (Gal. 1:16; 2:7-9; Rom. 11:13; 15:15f.), affirmed that the Gospel "is the power of God for salvation to every one who has faith, **to the Jew first** and also to the Greek" (Rom. 1:16). At the same time, "every human being who does evil, **the Jew first** and also the Greek," invites the displeasure of God upon himself (Rom. 2:9). Consequently, there can be no question of favoritism on God's part. Again, nothing could have been more natural than for Jerusalem, the very center and heart of Jewry, to be, as it was, the cradle of Christianity.

The first Christian believers, accordingly, were Jews; but it is also true that in the early years the fiercest opposition to the Gospel came from the Jews. In Pisidian Antioch, for example, antagonistic Jews "were filled with jealousy, and contradicted what was spoken by Paul, and reviled him"; and their hostility called forth this rejoinder from Paul and Barnabas:

> "It was necessary that the word of God should be spoken first to you. Since you thrust it from you, and judge yourselves unworthy of eternal life, behold we turn to the Gentiles. For so the Lord has commanded us, saying, 'I have set you to be a light for the Gentiles, that you may bring salvation to the uttermost parts of the earth'" (Acts 13:45-47).

In contrast, of course, to the embittered attitude of these Jews in Pisidian Antioch was that of the thousands of Jews who from the day of Pentecost on gladly received the message of the Gospel in Jerusalem (see, for example, Acts 2:41; 4:4). Nor should the significance be overlooked of the fact that Paul, like the apostles whom Jesus had chosen before him and the other evangelists of the apostolic church, was himself a Jew, indeed "a Hebrew of the Hebrews" (Phil. 3:5) and "a Pharisee, the son of Pharisees" (Acts 23:6); for this means that the remarkable explosion of evangelism in the church's earliest days was entirely the work of Jews who had recognized in Jesus of Nazareth the promised Messiah and Saviour of the world.

"THE FULNESS OF THE GENTILES"

We have already remarked that in the purposes of God the Gospel was always intended to be universal in scope, and that this was stated with explicit clarity in the promise given to Abraham that in his seed all the nations of the earth would be blessed (Gen. 12:3; 18:18; 22:18; Gal. 3:8). Despite these plain words and the utterances of similar import in the writings of the prophets, the Jewish-Christians, including even the apostles, had considerable difficulty in adjusting to the new situation that faced them. Their whole background was one of withdrawal from the Gentiles; but now their Master's command was that, instead of holding themselves aloof, they should penetrate and mingle with all nations, and carry the message of redemption to the uttermost parts of the earth (Mt. 28:19f.; Acts 1:8). Even after Pentecost, Peter had to learn to exchange his negative attitude toward the Gentiles for a positive one and not to call common what God has cleansed (Acts 10:14f.; 11:1-18).

Although the ministry of Christ was concentrated

on Palestinian territory, his outlook extended to the whole world. This is evident not only from his final commission to his followers but also from the teaching that he gave prior to his death and resurrection. Thus, when his disciples inquired concerning the signs of his coming and of the close of the age, he replied: "This gospel of the kingdom will be preached **throughout the whole world,** as a testimony **to all nations,** and then the end will come" (Mt. 24:14; cf. Mk. 13:10). To this the assertion recorded in the Third Gospel corresponds:

> "Jerusalem will be trodden down by the Gentiles, *until the times of the Gentiles are fulfilled.* And there will be signs in sun and moon and stars, and upon the earth distress of nations in perplexity at the roaring of the sea and the waves, men fainting with fear and with foreboding of what is coming on the world; for the powers of the heavens will be shaken. And *then they will see the Son of man coming* in a cloud with power and great glory" (Lk. 21:24-27).

These passages enable us to understand what Paul means when he speaks of "the fulness of the Gentiles" (Rom. 11:25). The completion of the commission to proclaim the Gospel to every nation throughout the world will signify both the fulness of the Gentiles and the end of the age.

This being so, we can better understand the intense and energetic missionary zeal and indeed restlessness of the Apostle Paul, all of whose labors and journeyings were "for the sake of the gospel" (1 Cor. 9:23), because he regarded himself as "under obligation both to Greeks and to barbarians, both to the wise and to the foolish," and was eager, as he told those to whom he wrote in Rome, "to reap some harvest among them as well as among the rest of the Gentiles" (Rom. 1:13-15). "If I preach the gospel," he writes to his Corinthian converts, "that gives me no ground for boasting. For necessity is laid upon me. Woe to me if I do not preach the gospel!" (1 Cor. 9:16).

It is because he desires to hasten the realization of the fulness of the Gentiles that he makes it his "ambition to preach the gospel where Christ has not already been named." Conscious of his own weakness, he says: "I will not venture to speak of anything except what Christ has wrought through me to win obedience from the Gentiles, by word and deed"; and at the time of his letter to the Romans he felt able to affirm: "From Jerusalem and as far round as Illyricum I have fully preached [literally, fulfilled] the gospel of Christ" (Rom. 15:18-20). What is to **fulfil the Gospel** in any place if not to advance a stage toward the fulness of the Gentiles? Paul adds, accordingly, that he hopes to see the Christians in Rome in passing as he travels on westward as far as Spain (Rom. 15:24, 28). It is of interest to find Clement of Rome stating, in his letter to the Corinthians, which was written before the close of the first century, that Paul "taught righteousness to the whole world, and reached the farthest limit of the west." The apostle's mission field was indeed the whole world. That is why he speaks of "the divine office" which was given to him "to make the word of God fully known" — or, literally, **"to fulfil the word of God"** (Col. 1:25), which is the same as "to fulfil the gospel" (Rom. 15:19), or, in other words, to bring in the fulness of the Gentiles.

Paul, it seems, was not without hope that the evangelization of the world for the bringing in of the fulness of the Gentiles, and with it the return of Christ in glory, might be completed in his own lifetime. There are several passages which suggest that he entertained this as a possibility. "We shall not all sleep, but we shall all be changed," he tells the believers in Corinth; at the sound of the last trumpet "the dead will be raised imperishable, and we shall be changed" (1 Cor. 15:51f.). To the Thessalonian Christians, troubled that death had overtaken some of their number, he writes that the Lord at his coming will bring with him "those who have fallen asleep," assuring them that "we who are alive, who are left until the coming of the Lord, shall not precede those who have fallen asleep"; for on that day when Christ descends from heaven "the dead in Christ will rise first," and "then we who are alive, who are left, shall be caught up together with them in the clouds to meet the Lord in the air; and so shall we always be with the Lord" (1 Thess. 4:13-17). Paul longs for the glorification of redeemed humanity which will take place when Christ comes, and would prefer not to experience the temporary nakedness that results from the separation of the soul from the body at death, though this does not mean separation from the Lord (2 Cor. 5:1-9). And always he must have had it in mind that the sooner the evangelization of the world was completed the sooner would the return of Christ take place.

We cite Paul because we have so much knowledge of his mind and work from his letters and from the Acts of the Apostles; but it must be remembered that he was only one of a multitude of ardent evangelists who were energetically carrying the Christian message to ever more distant territories. The movement had started before Paul's conversion when the thousands who had been won to the faith in Jerusalem were scattered by persecution and "went about preaching the word" (Acts 8:1, 4), so that their scattering meant the scattering of the good seed further and further afield. Thomas, for example, is said to have penetrated with the Gospel as far as India and to have suffered martyrdom there after founding a church which, it is claimed, has continued in existence to the present day.

In the midst of this remarkable evangelistic activity, then, Paul is able to write to the Colossians of his joy that the Gospel had come to them, "as indeed **in the whole world it is bearing fruit and growing**" (Col. 1:6); and these years of the apostolic period were indeed outstanding for the intense zeal and dedication with

which the task of proclaiming the Gospel was pros-
ecuted. That there should have been hopes of complet-
ing that task within a single generation was quite
understandable, and a tribute to the grand vision which
made the Church of Christ in those days so vital and
dynamic a fellowship. Moreover, this missionary enter-
prise was fundamentally the work of Jewish believers.

"THE FULNESS OF ISRAEL"

In Romans 11:17ff. the apostle Paul introduces the
analogy or parable of an olive tree for the purpose of
clarifying the relationship that exists between Jew and
Gentile. The **root** of the tree is the covenant God made
with Abraham and the promises associated with it.
The **richness** or **fatness** of the tree is the grace of God
mediated to men through Jesus Christ, in whom the
covenant and its promises come to fruition. The
branches of the tree are designated under two class-
ifications: first, the **natural** branches, which denote
Abraham's physical descendants; and, secondly, the
wild branches, which signify Gentile believers who are
grafted in so that they too may share in the tree's
richness. It is because of unbelief that natural branches
are broken off, and because of faith that wild branches
are grafted in. But all is the work of God, for it is God
who, as the great Husbandman (cf. 1 Cor. 3:5-9),
breaks off, and God who grafts in. There is a similar
analogy in John's Gospel, where Christ says to his
apostles: "I am the true vine, and my Father is the
vinedresser. . . . I am the vine, you are the branches.
He who abides in me, and I in him, he it is that bears
much fruit, for apart from me you can do nothing. If

a man does not abide in me, he is cast forth as a branch and withers" (Jn. 15:1ff.).

It is faith, then, that connects one to the grace which flows through the trunk of God's olive tree, and unbelief that severs this connection. If the Jewish people in general have been cut off because of their unbelief, this does not mean that there is no possibility that they, as the natural branches, should be "grafted back into their own olive tree"; for "if they do not persist in their unbelief they will be grafted in, for God has the power to graft them in again." Their restoration, indeed, would bring great blessing to the world (Rom. 11:15). As things are, a "partial hardening has come upon Israel until the fulness of the Gentiles comes in; and so," Paul adds, "all Israel will be saved" (vv. 25f.). The expression **all Israel** in this passage is the equivalent of **the fulness of Israel** of which the apostle speaks in verse 12. The fulness of the Gentiles and the fulness of Israel are two coordinate concepts, and the interpretation of the one should correspond with that of the other.

We have seen that the fulness of the Gentiles will be attained when the evangelization of all peoples in every corner of the world has been completed. It is by evangelization, too, that the fulness of Israel will be achieved. The two enterprises, in fact, overlap each other and provide mutual stimulation. The vigorous promotion of the missionary task of proclaiming Christ to all nations throughout the world will serve to bring enlightenment also to the heart of the Jewish people and to convince them that God who is rich in mercy to every Gentile believer is waiting to bestow the treasures of his grace in Christ upon them as well. And at the same time the acknowledgment by many Jews of Jesus as their true Messiah and Saviour will mean the release of powerful spiritual blessing for the world. That the attainment of the fulness of the Gentiles will coincide with the attainment of the fulness of Israel is indicated by the explanatory statement, "and so all Israel will be saved." The double goal will be reached at the same moment, which will also be the moment of Christ's return. Paul desired to see this fulfilment in his day, and we should desire to see it in ours; but the desire must be accompanied by an intensity of evangelistic zeal comparable to that of the apostolic age.

There are some who have supposed that Paul's expectation of the salvation of "all Israel," or "the fulness of Israel," implies that he looked for (and that we should also look for) the conversion to the Christian faith of the totality of the Jewish people prior to the return of Christ. But consistency of interpretation would then demand that they should understand "the fulness of the Gentiles" to mean the conversion of the totality of the Gentiles. This conclusion, however, they find unacceptable, if only because it would involve a universalism which is foreign both to the context — speaking as it does of the severity as well as of the kindness of God and of the breaking off of branches because of unbelief as well as of the grafting in of branches through faith (Rom. 11:17-22) — and to the teaching of Scripture as a whole. The scope of the Gospel of God's grace is universal but not universalistic (Rom. 10:11ff.).

Moreover, the totality of the Jewish people who happen to be alive at the time of Christ's return would not be, strictly speaking, all Israel, but only, so to say, the tip of the national iceberg, the main mass of which, consisting of the multitude, now dead, of those who belonged to the long line of the preceding generations, is invisible. These past generations would have every right to claim membership of "all Israel" and to protest their exclusion from it. The assembling of the totality of the people of Israel, from every corner of the earth and from every century of history, has in fact been a traditional expectation of Judaism. But it is not this totality of which Paul is speaking. He has argued, on the basis of the scriptural evidence, that "all Israel" does not mean all Israelites (Rom. 9:6f.), that the genuine Jew is not the one who conforms to outward conventions but the one who inwardly, in the heart, has experienced the regenerating touch of the Spirit of God (Rom. 2:28f.), and that the instrument of God's purposes is "a remnant, chosen by grace" (Rom. 11:5).

"All Israel" or "the fulness of Israel," then, is the full number of those Jews (the terms "Israel" and "Jews" are used interchangeably by Paul) who by God's grace hear and by faith receive the message of the Gospel; and "the fulness of the Gentiles," likewise, is the full number of Gentile believers from every nation under the sun. In both cases the "fulness" implies the completion of the worldwide task of evangelism in preparation for the return of Christ. Together, however, they constitute **one fulness,** not two, the fulness, namely, of Christ: that innumerable multitude of the redeemed which eternally is one in him (Rev. 7:9ff.), "the church, which is his body, **the fulness of him who fills all in all**" (Eph. 1:22f.). The Gentiles, like the younger son in the parable who had squandered his goods in a far country, find, undeserving though they are, that through Christ there is a welcome for them in the Father's home. But the family circle is not complete until the Jews, who, like the elder brother, are resentful at the wideness of God's mercy, are persuaded to come in and rejoice with the whole household over the rebirth of the son that was dead and the finding of him that was lost, and thus to cease excluding themselves from the blessings of the new covenant (Lk. 15:11ff.). The joy of this great family reunion in which the ancient animosity is replaced by the sublime harmony of our perfect oneness in Christ is nowhere better expressed than in the words written by the apostle Paul to the Gentile Christians in Ephesus:

96

Remember that you were at one time separated from Christ, alienated from the commonwealth of Israel, and strangers to the covenants of promise, having no hope and without God in the world. But now in Christ Jesus you who once were far off have been brought near in the blood of Christ. For he is our peace, *who has made us both one,* and has broken down the dividing wall of hostility, by abolishing in his flesh the law of commandments and ordinances, that he might create *in himself one new man in place of the two,* so making peace, and might *reconcile us both to God in one body* through the cross, thereby bringing the hostility to an end. And he came and preached peace to you who were far off [that is, Gentiles] and peace to those who were near [that is, Jews]; for *through him we both have access in one Spirit to the Father.* So then you are no longer strangers and sojourners, but you are fellow citizens with the saints and *members of the household of God* (Eph. 2:11-19).

THE MILLENNIAL REIGN

In Revelation 20:1ff. John describes a vision in which he saw certain events associated with a millennium or period of one thousand years. That this is a difficult passage is indicated by the great divergence of opinion concerning its interpretation. Yet despite the problems it presents, and although this is the only place in Scripture where this period of a thousand years is mentioned, it has frequently been treated as a key to the understanding of other prophetic passages, particularly in the Old Testament, or as a foundation on which elaborate eschatological superstructures have been built. But before we enter into a discussion of the passage and its meaning let us set down what the text says:

Then I saw an angel coming down from heaven holding in his hand the key of the bottomless pit and a great chain. And he seized the dragon, that ancient serpent, who is the Devil and Satan, and bound him for *a thousand years*, and threw him into the pit, and shut it and sealed it over him, that he should deceive the nations no more, till *the thousand years* were ended. After that he must be loosed for a little while. Then I saw thrones, and seated on them were those to whom judgment was committed. And I also saw the souls of those who had been beheaded for their testimony to Jesus and for the word of God, and who had not worshipped the beast or its image and had not received its mark on their foreheads or on their hands. They lived and reigned with Christ *a thousand years*. The rest of the dead did not live until *the thousand years* were ended. This is the first resurrection. Blessed and holy is he who shares in the first resurrection! Over such the second death has no power, but they shall be priests of God and of Christ, and they shall reign with him *a thousand years*. And when *the thousand years* are ended, Satan will be loosed from his prison and will come out to deceive the nations which are at the four corners of the earth, that is, Gog and Magog, to gather them for battle; their number is like the sand of the sea. And they marched up over the broad earth and surrounded the camp of the saints and the beloved city; but fire came down from heaven and consumed them, and the devil who had deceived them was thrown into the lake of fire and brimstone where the beast and the false prophet were, and they will be tormented day and night for ever and ever (Rev. 20:1-10).

The verses that follow depict the judgment of the dead before the great white throne and the consignment of all whose names were not found written in the book of life to the same destruction as had been meted out to the Devil (20:11-15). Then comes the vision of the everlasting bliss of the new heaven and the new earth (21:1ff.).

The major division of opinion concerning the interpretation of the passage we have quoted is between those who maintain that the return of Christ will take place **before** the reign of a thousand years (the premillennial view) and those who hold that it will take place **after** the reign of a thousand years (the postmillennial view). It should be mentioned also that in Jewish expectation there was the anticipation of a final golden age which would be the seventh or sabbath day of human history, lasting a thousand years (though the estimates of the length of its duration did in fact vary), and in which Gentile domination would be put down and the messianic kingdom established with a resplendent Jerusalem as its capital and the magnificence of the temple and its priesthood restored. To return to Christian interpretations, the postmillennial viewpoint envisages the millennium as a period at the end of this present age when the Christian church will flourish and the Gospel be widely accepted — in other words, a golden age in which Christ will reign through his church now dominant after centuries of suffering and ignominy. This viewpoint, one must say, seems to underestimate the achievements of divine power and the conquests of divine grace in the history of the church (admittedly weak in itself), and also to overlook the witness of the New Testament that the latter part of this age will see not a decrease but an intensification of the power of evil in the world, which, however, will in no way imply a defeat for the church or for the purposes of God. Furthermore, if a season of supremacy for the church must intervene before the return of Christ, this would seem to nullify the emphasis placed, as we have seen, by Christ and his apostles on the imminence of his return and the importance of being constantly watchful lest it should find us careless and unprepared.

Another perspective, which might also be classified as postmillennial but which is now commonly designated amillennial (inaccurately, because it does not dismiss the "thousand years" of Revelation 20 as

99

non-existent), is that of those who, understanding the number 1,000 to have a symbolical force, interpret the millennium as virtually synonymous with this present age between the two comings of Christ, or, more precisely, between the coronation of the ascended Saviour and his return in glory. This position we believe to be most in accord with the perspective of the New Testament, as we shall endeavor shortly to demonstrate.

According to what may be called the classic premillennial view, the second coming of Christ will see the resurrection of the saints and their participation in the kingdom which he will then establish on earth and which will endure for a thousand years. At the end of this period there will come the last paroxysm of Satan and his armies, and their total defeat will be followed by final judgment and the renewal of creation. There were some who conceived the delights of the millennium in a manner that was carnal rather than spiritual. The first-century heretic Cerinthus, for example, against whose teachings the writings of the apostle John were intended as an antidote, described it as a period of fleshly desires and pleasures, and especially of marriage festivals (see Eusebius, **Church History** iii. 28) ; and early in the second century Papias, Bishop of Hierapolis, propounded the fanciful notion that the millennial vegetation would be so exuberant that each vine would have ten thousand branches, each branch ten thousand twigs, each twig ten thousand shoots, each shoot ten thousand clusters, each cluster ten thousand grapes, and that each grape would yield twenty-five measures of wine (see Irenaeus, **Against Heresies** v. 33) !

That judgments differed from early times over the interpretation of the "thousand years" is evident from a statement made by Justin Martyr in the middle of the second century. "I and others, who are right-minded Christians on all points," he wrote, "are assured that there will be a resurrection of the dead and a thousand years in Jerusalem, which will then be built, adorned, and enlarged, as the prophets Ezekiel and Isaiah and others declare"; but in the same place he asserts that "many who belong to the pure and pious faith and are true Christians think otherwise" (**Dialogue with Trypho** 80f.). The clearest declaration of premillennial doctrine (though not necessarily the most orthodox) that survives from the early centuries comes from the pen of Lactantius, writing in the first decades of the fourth century:

Peace once secured, and all evil overthrown, the righteous and victorious prince will execute judgment on the living and the dead over all the earth; to the living righteous he will assign all nations for servitude, but the dead he will raise to eternal life, and will himself reign with them on earth and found a holy city. This kingdom of the saints will last a thousand years. During that same time the light of the stars will be magnified and the sun's brightness be increased and the light of the moon no longer suffer diminution. Then will come down from God showers of blessing, both morning and evening, while the earth will yield her fruits without toil on the part of mankind. Honey will drip from the rocks, fountains of milk and wine gush forth, wild beasts — laying aside their ferocity — will grow gentle, the wolf wandering harmless amid the flocks, the calf feeding with the lion, the dove consorting with the hawk, the snake losing its venom; no creature will then live by blood. For God will bestow on all creatures innocent food in abundance. But at the close of the thousand years, when the prince of the demons is unchained, the nations will renew warfare with the righteous and an innumerable multitude will come to storm the city of the saints. In that hour shall the last judgment of God be executed upon the nations. . . . For a brief while the righteous will lie hidden underground, until the nations come to perdition; then, after three days, they will issue forth and behold the plains covered with dead bodies. There will be an earthquake; mountains will be riven and the valleys sink into the depths. . . . After this God will renew the world and change the righteous into angelic shapes, that, being

101

clothed with the garment of immortality, they may serve God for ever. And this will be the Kingdom of God, and of that kingdom there shall be no end (*Epitome of the Divine Institutes* 72).

DISPENSATIONALISM

Very much more elaborate than anything known in the church until quite recent times is the convoluted eschatology of those who belong to the "dispensationalist" school. Many of these seem to regard the premillennial creed as an authenticating mark of those who are acceptable as fully orthodox. Indeed, it has become customary for dispensationalist authors to adduce the assertion of Justin Martyr (quoted above) — "I and others, who are right-minded Christians on all points, are assured that there will be a resurrection of the dead and a thousand years in Jerusalem" — as proof conclusive that premillennialism was "the criterion of a perfect orthodoxy" in the post-apostolic church, though they can do so only by the really inexcusable suppression of Justin's qualification in the same passage, namely, that "many who belong to the pure and pious faith and are true Christians think otherwise." No more impressive is it to cite the names of liberals, romanists, and unitarians whose outlook has been other than premillennial, as though this suffices to demonstrate that premillennialism and soundness of faith belong inseparably together. The device of guilt by association proves nothing and can readily become a boomerang, since it is easy to retort that the premillennial position has also been that of heretics and deviant sects, from Cerinthus in the time of the apostles to the Mormons and Jehovah's Witnesses in our day. But this is the way of pride and triumphalism, and it ill becomes those who ought humbly to be seeking an understanding of the sacred text.

Briefly, it is the contention of dispensationalists that the Old Testament did not foresee or foretell the coming of this present age of the Christian church, but that its expectation was focused on the setting up of the messianic kingdom which would be the proper inheritance of the Israelites, or physical descendants of Abraham, as distinct from the Gentiles, though blessings were intended for the latter also; that the teaching of Jesus concerning the kingdom, whether in parables or other forms of discourse, was directed exclusively to the Jews; that the Jews turned away from the kingdom that was then offered to them, with the result that the offer was withdrawn and the establishment of the kingdom postponed to a later occasion; that meanwhile the period of the church was inaugurated as a "parenthesis" in the divinely revealed sequence of events, but a period which, as we have indicated, is outside the scope of biblical prophecy and to which Christ's kingdom teaching has no application; that at the close of this church age Christ will come for his saints, who will be caught up to meet him in the air; that there will follow an interval of seven years during the first half of which many Israelites will accept Jesus as their Saviour and Messiah and will carry out a massive program for the evangelization of the world, while the latter three-and-a-half years will be a time of intense persecution known as "the great tribulation"; that at the end of these seven years Christ will come again, this time not for but with his saints (this event generally being described as his second coming proper), in order to reign upon earth for one thousand years; that thus, the church parenthesis now a thing of the past, the prophecies of the messianic kingdom will achieve fulfilment and his own kingdom teaching be observed; that, with a resplendent Jerusalem as his capital, the temple demarcated by Ezekiel will be constructed and the levitical priesthood and sacrifices reinstituted; and that in this millennium of peace, order, and prosperity his sovereignty over all the earth will be established for all to see.

Such are the anticipations of dispensationalists. There are of course many more details and intricacies that could be added, and it is not surprising that there are numerous differences of opinion on matters of interpretation and the manner of the outworking of their scheme. Our purpose in writing this essay is not polemical, however, and we do not intend to discuss these divergences here. But we fear that the dispensationalist method of interpretation does violence to the unity of Scripture and to the sovereign continuity of God's purposes, and cavalierly leaves out of account a major portion of the apostolic teaching — that, chiefly, of the Acts and the Epistles — as unrelated to the perspective of the Old Testament authors. We shall limit ourselves here to a consideration of the premillennial conception of the significance of the thousand years, and shall also attempt to set forth our own understanding of the meaning of Revelation 20:1ff., which all, surely, must admit holds a number of difficulties for the interpreter.

PROPHECY AND THE CHURCH

Is this church period a parenthesis, a stop-gap, made necessary by the contingency of the rejection by the Jews of the kingdom at Christ's first coming? Would that kingdom have been set up on earth there and then if their response had been positive? Was God's position one of doubt and uncertainty, so that he had to wait and see what the answer of the Jews would be? And when it turned out to be a negative answer was he forced to resort to an emergency measure until such time as he could put his original plan into effect? We may assume that it is not the intention of dispensationalists to diminish the competence and sovereignty of Almighty God and the immutability of his purposes; but their explanation of the sequence of events can hardly fail to arouse questions such as these. Indeed, this mentality seems to be little removed from that of Roman Catholic apologists who defend the notion of Mary as co-redemptrix with Christ, or at least as the one who shares with God the credit for mankind's salvation, on the ground that the incarnation was contingent on her giving an affirmative response to the angel of the annunciation (Lk. 1:38, "Let it be to me according to your word").

Certainly, the apostles do not appear to have regarded the era of the church as a parenthesis outside the scope of the prophetic vision. On the Day of Pentecost, for example, Peter assures his large Jewish audience that the sending forth of the Holy Spirit is "what was spoken by the prophet Joel," through whom God declared that in the last days he would pour out his Spirit upon all flesh, with the consequence that "whoever calls on the name of the Lord shall be saved" (Joel 2:28-32); that Jesus of Nazareth was delivered up to be crucified "according to the definite plan and foreknowledge of God," and was raised to life again in fulfilment of what "David says concerning him" in Psalm 16; and that his ascension to God's right hand has brought to pass the prophetic words of David in Psalm 110. "Let all the house of Israel therefore know assuredly," he concludes, "that God has made him both Lord and Messiah, this Jesus whom you crucified" (Acts 2:14-36). Neither here nor elsewhere is there any mention of a postponement of the kingdom or a change of plan on God's part. Quite the contrary, for all that they are witnessing is in accordance with the predetermined purpose of God and the prophetic utterances of the Old Testament writers. On that historic day some three thousand Jews welcomed the message proclaimed by Peter and were baptized (Acts 2:41).

Shortly afterward, in an apostolic prayer-meeting, recognition is expressed of the fact that fierce opposition to the Gospel (in this church age!) was foretold by David in Psalm 2 and that all the hostile forces that had gathered together to destroy Jesus succeeded in doing only "whatever thy hand and thy plan had predestined to take place" (Acts 4:23-28). Similarly, Paul, formerly the proud Pharisee and persecutor of the church, preaches the fulfilment of the Old Testament scriptures in the blessings of this present church age, including "the holy and sure blessings of David," which, being the blessings **of David,** must be **kingdom** blessings:

> "We bring you the good news that *what God promised to the fathers, this he has fulfilled* to us their children by raising Jesus; as also it is written in the second psalm, 'Thou art my Son, today I have begotten thee.' And as for the fact that he raised him from the dead, no more to return to corruption, he spoke in this way, 'I will give you the holy and sure blessings of David.' Therefore he says also in another psalm, 'Thou wilt not let thy Holy One see corruption' " (Acts 13:32-35).

And, significantly, Paul goes on to warn his Jewish audience (in Pisidian Antioch) that rejection of the message of the Gospel will bring upon them the disaster foretold by the prophets of old:

> "Beware, therefore, lest there come upon you what is said in the prophets: 'Behold, you scoffers, and wonder, and perish; for I do a deed in your days, a deed you will never believe, if one declares it to you' " (Acts 13:40f.; Hab. 1:5).

106

At the first council of the Christian church, commonly known as the Council of Jerusalem, which is described by Luke in Acts 15, called for the purpose of resolving certain questions concerning the position of Gentile believers and the relevance of Judaism to Christian faith and practice, James, the brother of Jesus, addressed the assembly as its president, pointing out that God's calling of a people for his name from among the Gentiles was in accord with the prophetic scriptures:

> "*With this the words of the prophets agree,* as it is written, 'After this I will return and will rebuild the dwelling of David, which has fallen; I will rebuild its ruins, and I will set it up, that the rest of men may seek the Lord, and all the Gentiles who are called by my name, *says the Lord, who has made these things known from of old*'" (Acts 15:15-18; see Amos 9:11f.; Is. 55:5; 45:21).

Here is another remarkable instance of a "kingdom" passage, relating to "the dwelling of David," being interpreted in the most authoritative manner as finding its fulfilment in the events of this church age. Plainly, this synod of apostles and elders (Acts 15:6), whose judgment was expressed by James, understood the rebuilding of David's house to be accomplished in God's building of his church — a structure which, as we have already seen, Peter would describe in a manner entirely consonant with the interpretation of the Council of Jerusalem, of which he was a prominent member, as composed of the "living stones" of believers, "built into a spiritual house, to be a holy priesthood, to offer spiritual sacrifices, acceptable to God through Jesus Christ" (1 Pet. 2:5).

If there is a difference between the "kingdom" and the "church," the apostles and evangelists of the New Testament seem to have been unaware of it. The "good news" preached by the "deacon" Philip in Samaria was

107

"about the kingdom of God and the name of Jesus Christ" (Acts 8:12) ; and Paul spent three months in Ephesus "arguing and pleading about the kingdom of God" in the synagogue there (Acts 19:8; cf. 20:25). This is Paul's theme again when, during his first captivity in Rome, he called together the local leaders of the Jews and explained to them that it was **"because of the hope of Israel"** that he was in bonds, and subsequently expounded the Gospel to them "from morning till evening, **testifying to the kingdom of God** and trying to convince them about Jesus **both from the law of Moses and from the prophets"** (Acts 28:17-20, 23 ; cf. 24:14). It was, indeed, precisely "for hope in the promise made by God to our fathers, to which our twelve tribes hope to attain, as they earnestly worship night and day," that the apostle, as he told King Agrippa, had been brought to trial by his fellow Jews (Acts 26:6f.). In the light of such evidence it must surely be clear that in the apostolic doctrine and preaching the church could not possibly have been regarded as a parenthesis hidden from the perspective of the writers of the Old Testament.

This conclusion is confirmed by the readiness with which the apostolic authors of the New Testament epistles cite the ancient promises given to Israel in order to show that it is in Jesus Christ and his church that they find their fulfilment. In Christ, Paul assures the Gentile believers in Corinth and Achaia, "all the promises of God find their Yes. That is why [in our worship] we utter the Amen through him, to the glory of God" (2 Cor. 1:20). Thus to them, Gentile members of the Christian church, he applies God's promise spoken to Israel through Moses and in later days repeated by the prophets as an essential element of the future new covenant: "I will live in them and move among them, and I will be their God and they shall be my people" (see Lev. 26:12; Ex. 25:8; 29:45; Jer. 30:22; 31:33; Ezek. 11:20; 37:26f., etc.) ; and it is precisely on such passages that he bases his admonition to them not to compromise with unbelief, since "we are the temple of the living God" (2 Cor. 6:14-16).

The same is true, of course, of Jewish believers whose faith in Christ has likewise brought them into membership of the Christian church. The author of the Epistle to the Hebrews, for example, informs his readers that the new covenant foretold by the prophets — new, that is, in relation to the Mosaic covenant which was in force in their day — is fulfilled in Christ who is the mediator of this new and better covenant (Heb. 8:6; 9:15; 12:24). The church of Christ, accordingly, is the sphere of the new covenant, and the blessings of this covenant are bestowed on the members of the church, as summed up in the promise, "I will put my laws in their minds, and write them on their hearts, and I will be their God, and they shall be my people," while the full realization of all that is promised awaits the eternal perfection of the new heaven and the new earth. But the most significant consideration for our present argument is that though the promise of a new covenant was announced to Israel and Judah — "The days will come, says the Lord, when I will establish a new covenant with the house of Israel and with the house of Judah" — yet it comes to fruition in "the church of the Lord which he purchased with his own blood" (Acts 20:28), the blood, namely, of the new covenant (Heb. 8:6-13; 9:11-15; 10:29; 13:20; cf. 1 Cor. 11:25; Mt. 26:28; Mk. 14:22).

THE BINDING OF SATAN

The text of Revelation 20:1-10 has been given above

(p. 98), and some of the important problems it poses for the interpreter must now be considered. In the first place, John describes the **binding of Satan,** who is seized and thrown into the bottomless pit and there secured and sealed for a thousand years (vv. 1f.). The premillennialist takes this to mean that for the period of one thousand years when Christ, following his second coming, reigns on earth Satan will be immobilized and placed under duress, thus ensuring that this will be a time of peace and blessedness unspoiled by his activities. The purpose of Satan's binding, however, is defined as being in particular **"that he should deceive the nations no more,** till the thousand years were ended" (v. 3) ; and this is better understood, within the perspective of the New Testament, as referring to the present "times of the Gentiles" when the Devil is held under restraint as the Gospel is preached to all nations.

The advent of Christ has brought about a change in the relationship between Satan and the nations. "In past generations God allowed **all the nations** to walk in their own ways," Paul told the Gentile crowd at Lystra. But now things are different. That is why he and Barnabas had come to the Gentile territory of Lycaonia and were pleading with them to turn from their vain superstitions to the living God who is the Creator of all (Acts 14:15f.). Later, when he came to Greece, the apostle announced this same change in the situation of the nations to the intellectual audience that had gathered to hear him in Athens. Hitherto, he tells them, "God has overlooked the times of ignorance," that is to say, the times of **Gentile** ignorance, during which, so to speak, the nations were in the wings and only the people of Israel were on stage; "but now," he adds, "he commands **all men everywhere** to repent." Why? Because since the advent of Christ, in whom there is blessing for every nation on earth, for Gentile as well as Jew, all men have been brought fully into the scene and it is by him that God "will judge the world in righteousness" (Acts 17:30f.).

Prior to the coming of Christ the nations had been permitted to remain in the darkness and ignorance of that superstition which resulted from Satan's deception. They had "walked in their own ways." In striking contrast to this, Israel alone of all the peoples on earth had been entrusted with the oracles of God (Rom. 3:2); they had the knowledge and the enlightenment which God's revelation brings; and therefore it was required of them that they should be altogether distinct from the nations precisely by walking, not in their own ways (which would be to imitate the nations), but in God's ways (cf. Dt. 5:32f.; 10:12; 12:1ff., etc.). "You are a people holy to the Lord your God," Moses reminded them, "and the Lord has chosen you to be a people for his own possession, out of all the peoples that are on the face of the earth" (Dt. 14:2) — but God's choosing of the Israelites was, as we have earlier observed, for the purpose of bringing blessing to all the nations of the earth, and that purpose has been achieved in and through the coming of Christ.

No longer, then, are the nations left in the shadows. No longer is Satan permitted to blind the nations with his deception. For God's salvation has been "prepared in the presence of all peoples" and Christ is "a light to lighten the nations" as well as the glory of God's people Israel (Lk. 2:30-32). Christ's witnesses are now to proclaim the gospel message to the farthest parts of the earth so that the fulness of the nations may be brought in (Mt. 24:14; Rom. 11:25). The power of Satan over the nations has been broken by the power of the Gospel. The darkness of his deception is dispelled by the light of him who declared, "I am the Light of the world" (Jn. 8:12; 9:5). Thus the presence of Jesus in "Galilee of the nations" means for Matthew the fulfilment of the words spoken by the prophet Isaiah: "The people who sat in darkness have seen a great light, and for those who sat in the region and shadow of death light has dawned" (Mt. 4:13-16; Is. 9:1f.).

In Revelation 20:2f. the binding of Satan is specifically limited in reference to his deceiving of the nations. The considerations we have given point to the reason for this particular sphere of reference. His binding, therefore, does not preclude the possibility of his continuing activity in the world within the lives of individuals or of society in general. As "the god of this world" his evil work is apparent in his "blinding of the minds of unbelievers, to keep them from seeing the light of the gospel of the glory of Christ" (2 Cor. 4:4). He is still "our adversary the devil" who "prowls around like a roaring lion, seeking someone to devour" (1 Pet. 5:8). But his binding in relation to the nations is nonetheless real as the Gospel multiplies its conquests throughout the world.

THE STRONG MAN BOUND

We have seen that the incarnation of the Son of God for the purpose of redeeming the world has produced a new situation in which the Gentiles are now brought fully into the picture. That they were always in the picture so far as the divine intention is concerned is shown by the promise given to Abraham that in his seed all the nations of the earth would be blessed, and from the numerous predictions of the prophets that God's grace would flow to all the families of mankind. God's purpose of universal blessing is described by Paul as a **mystery** which has become fully clear only with the coming of Christ — for by this use of the term "mystery" the apostle speaks of an age-old purpose

112

of God, which for centuries has remained hidden or but partially disclosed, but now is plainly revealed for all to see. Through the shedding of Christ's blood the Gentiles, who previously were "alienated from the commonwealth of Israel and strangers to the covenants of promise," in short were **far off**, have been **brought near.** Christ is "our peace," who has made Jew and Gentile one, because "he has broken down the dividing wall of hostility." In him, accordingly, the nations are "no longer strangers and sojourners," but are "fellow citizens with the saints and members of the household of God" (Eph. 2:11ff.). This is the mystery now made known by revelation —

> the mystery of Christ, which was not made known to the sons of men in other generations as it has now been revealed to his holy apostles and prophets by the Spirit; that is, how the Gentiles are fellow heirs, members of the same body, and partakers of the promise in Christ Jesus through the gospel.

And "this was according to the eternal purpose which God has realized in Christ Jesus our Lord" (Eph. 3:3ff.).

When the scribes accused Jesus of being "possessed by Beelzebul" and of casting out demons by "the prince of demons," he responded by pointing out that this amounted to an absurd proposition, namely, that Satan was casting out Satan. The only reasonable conclusion, which they were unwilling to draw, was that it was by the Spirit of God that he was casting out demons, and therefore that the power of God was manifestly at work in their midst. Did they really think that Satan could be fighting against himself? And then he added: "No one can enter a strong man's house and plunder his goods, unless **he first binds the strong man**; then indeed he may plunder his house" (Mk. 3:22ff.; Mt. 12:24ff.). Christ's casting out of demons was an evidence not only that the strong man's house was being plundered but also that Satan had been bound. Christ is the one who is stronger than Satan, and that is why, when the seventy whom he had sent out returned rejoicing that even the demons were subject to them in his name, he could say to them: "I saw Satan fall like lightning from heaven. Behold, **I have given you authority over all the power of the enemy**" (Lk. 10:17-19; 11:21f.). That is why, as he approached the ordeal and the victory of the cross, he could declare: "Now is the judgment of this world, now shall the ruler of this world be cast out; and I, when I am lifted up from the earth, will draw all men to myself" (Jn. 12:31f.) — for the binding of Satan that he should deceive the nations no more makes possible the casting of the gospel net over **all men.** That is why, again, the risen Lord can encourage his apostles and commission them with these words: "**All authority in heaven and on earth has been given to me.** Go therefore and **make disciples of all nations**" (Mt. 28:18f.). With Satan effectively bound, and all authority concentrated in Christ, their evangelical charge is one that leads them to all the nations of the world.

Paul writes to similar effect in the Epistle to the Colossians, when he says that God "disarmed the principalities and powers and made a public example of them, triumphing over them in Christ's cross" (Col. 2:15); and in the Epistle to the Hebrews there is, if anything, an even more explicit statement where the writer asserts that in the incarnation the Son of God partook of our human nature, "in order that through death he might render ineffective him who has the power of death, that is, the devil, and deliver all those who through fear of death were subject to lifelong bondage" (Heb. 2:14f.). There is also a passage in the Revelation which seems to have a bearing on this interpretation of the binding of Satan. It is generally agreed that this passage (ch. 12:1ff.) refers to the birth, death, and exaltation of Christ and to the over-

114

throw of Satan which these events effected. John sees a woman in the pangs of childbirth and a dragon waiting to devour her child when it is born; she gives birth to a male child "who is to rule **all the nations** with a rod of iron," but the dragon fails in his design because "her child was caught up to God and to his throne"; there follows an account of war in heaven in which the dragon and his angels are defeated, "and the great dragon, that ancient serpent, who is called the Devil and Satan, **the deceiver of the whole world**, was thrown down to the earth," and his angels with him; and this calls forth the joyful proclamation: "Now **the salvation** and **the power** and **the kingdom of our God** and **the authority of his Christ** have come!" His mission to earth completed, the Redeemer of mankind assumes all authority as the ruler of "all the nations," while Satan, "the deceiver of the whole world," is overthrown and the peoples of the world are released from his domination. Or, in the words of Revelation 20:2f., "the dragon, that ancient serpent, who is the Devil and Satan," has been "seized" and "bound" and "thrown into the pit," which has been "shut and sealed over him," "so that he should deceive the nations no more, till the thousand years are ended." At the end of that period, we are advised, "he must be loosed for a little while."

REIGNING WITH CHRIST

Our attempt to understand the significance of the binding of Satan, as described in the opening verses of Revelation 20, in accordance with the teaching given elsewhere in the New Testament has led us to the conclusion that this binding, the particular purpose of which was that Satan should deceive the nations no more till the thousand years were ended, was effected through the victorious ministry, sacrificial death, and exaltation of the incarnate Son. It follows, on this interpretation, that Satan is bound even now as the Gospel is universally proclaimed and that the millennium is not a future but a present reality. We have seen (pp. 25ff.) that the apostles taught plainly and insistently that, in fulfilment of the prophetic scriptures, the ascended Saviour is now reigning in glory at the right hand of the Majesty on high, and will continue to reign until all enemies have been placed under his feet (1 Cor. 15:24ff.; Heb. 2:9, etc.). This consideration strengthens the conclusion that this present age is the time of the millennium, for John explains that the thousand years of his vision is a period in which Christ is reigning (vv. 4 and 6).

It is, of course, as the **ascended** Lord that Christ is now crowned with glory and honor. His enthronement at the Father's right hand is **on high.** Now, obviously, our understanding that this is the millennial reign of Christ depicted by the seer is incompatible with the premillennial interpretation, according to which the thousand-year rule of Christ is not present but future, and is exercised not from heaven but on earth. Actually, there is no indication in the passage before us that Christ's millennial reign is or will be an **earthly** reign. Nor, for that matter, does it state that it is a **heavenly** reign; though, as we shall show, the context does support the rightness of the latter conclusion.

The apostle John writes that he "saw thrones" upon which were seated "those to whom judgment was committed"; and he goes on to designate more fully the identity of those who were thus enthroned, as follows:

I saw the souls of those who had been beheaded for

116

their testimony to Jesus and for the word of God, and who had not worshipped the beast and had not received its mark on their foreheads or their hands. They lived and reigned with Christ a thousand years (v. 4).

It is important to notice that he is speaking of **souls,** that is to say, persons who have died and are in the disembodied state. It is true that the Greek word translated "souls" here (**psychai**) is also used in the New Testament of persons who exist bodily on earth — as, for example, in Acts 2:41 where it is said that about three thousand souls were added to the number of believers on the Day of Pentecost, and in 1 Peter 3:20 where we read that eight souls were saved in the ark at the time of the flood. But this sense is inappropriate to the term in the present passage which is concerned with persons who have suffered physical death and yet who live and reign with Christ during the thousand years. This description of Christians who have departed this life corresponds with an earlier passage in which John tells how he saw "the souls of those who had been slain for the word of God and for the witness they had borne," and who cried out, "O Sovereign Lord, holy and true, how long before thou wilt judge and avenge our blood on those who dwell upon the earth?" (Rev. 6:9f.). Though killed, and no longer themselves dwelling upon earth, their souls were living in the divine presence.

Such language fits in well with the teaching of Paul that the Christian who has died is "away from the body and at home with the Lord" (2 Cor. 5:8), and that "to die is gain" because it means "to depart and be with Christ" (Phil. 1:21, 23). When speaking of those souls who live and reign with Christ during the millennium, John, apparently, is not speaking exclusively of those who have suffered martyrdom; for he envisages two groups of persons: (1) those "who had been beheaded for their testimony to Jesus and for the word of God," and (2) those "who had not worshipped the beast or its image and had not received its mark

117

on their foreheads or their hands" — those, in short, who have been faithful unto death (Rev. 2:10), whether that death be a violent one or not. This principle is well illustrated by the lives and deaths of the brothers James and John, who, when Jesus asked them, "Are you able to drink the cup that I drink, or to be baptized with the baptism with which I am baptized?", replied, "We are able," and to whom Jesus then said, "The cup that I drink you will drink, and with the baptism with which I am baptized you will be baptized" (Mk. 10:38f.). Such words speak of "the fellowship of Christ's sufferings" (Phil. 3:10) which is the very essence of Christian martyrdom, for Christian martyrdom means faithful witness to Christ not only in death but also in life. In the case of James and John, the former was the first of the apostles to be "martyred" (Acts 12:1f.), whereas the latter lived on into old age and did not "suffer a martyr's death"; yet he drank the cup of suffering and was baptized with the baptism of persecution no less than his brother. So also in John's vision the souls he sees reigning with Christ are the souls of those who have been faithful witnesses both in life and in death. They are a manifestation of the truth of the declaration, "Blessed are the dead who die in the Lord" (Rev. 14:13).

The blessedness of the dead who die in the Lord has already been affirmed, though in different words, in the earlier part of John's Revelation, where the members of the church in Ephesus are told that they must expect tribulation, but are encouraged with these words: "Be faithful unto death, and I will give you the crown of life," and with the assurance that "he who overcomes will not be hurt by the second death" (Rev. 2:10f.). This passage clearly has a close affinity with the millennial passage which we are discussing. The souls of those who die in the Lord, John teaches, live and reign with Christ a thousand years. These are the dead who in fact are living. With them the rest of the dead, that is, those who die in unbelief, have no part; they do not participate in what John calls **the first resurrection**, for what awaits them is the judgment of **the second death.** But, again (as in 14:13), the blessedness of the dead in the Lord is proclaimed: "Blessed and holy is he who shares in the first resurrection! Over such the second death has no power" (vv. 5f.).

THE FIRST RESURRECTION

We must now consider what is meant by "the first resurrection." In the first place, it must be emphasized again that in this passage the first resurrection is the blessed experience of the souls of those who are in Christ, and with Christ, though "dead and buried" as far as this world is concerned. It is not the experience of "the rest of the dead." Secondly, Scripture elsewhere contemplates **only one bodily resurrection** of the dead, which, because it involves the raising of all men, has customarily been known as the **general** resurrection. The Athanasian Creed, for example, after affirming Christ's ascension into heaven and his session at the right hand of the Father, "from whence he shall come to judge the quick and the dead," declares that at his coming "all men shall rise again with their bodies, and shall give account for their own works." This is a straightforward summary of the biblical doctrine. Thus in the book of Daniel we read that "those who sleep in the dust of the earth shall awake, some to everlasting life, and some to shame and everlasting contempt" (Dan. 12:2). Otherwise, however, the teaching of resurrection is not clearly developed in the Old Testament,

119

although there is a definite expectation of future life in the presence of God for those who fear him.

In the New Testament there is a great advance in the understanding of this subject, which is not surprising in view of the centrality in the gospel message of the bodily death and resurrection of Jesus. The general resurrection is explicitly announced by Christ himself in these words: "The hour is coming when all who are in the tombs will hear his voice and come forth, those who have done good to the resurrection of life, and those who have done evil to the resurrection of judgment" (Jn. 5:28f.). That this does not mean two resurrections, but one resurrection involving the classification of all into two groups, the justified and the wicked, so that the resurrection has a twofold outcome, either life or judgment, depending on which group one is in, is confirmed by the parable of the separation between the sheep and the goats at the return of Christ, the former passing into eternal life and the latter into eternal punishment (Mt. 25:31ff.), and by Paul's assertion that "there will be a resurrection of both the just and the unjust" (Acts 24:15). The reality of the resurrection is implicit also in Christ's admonition to his disciples that, rather than fearing men who can kill only the body, they should fear God "who can destroy both soul and body in hell" (Mt. 10:28).

Now it is evident that the persons whose souls live and reign with Christ during the millennium are awaiting the general resurrection, when the nakedness of separation from their bodies will cease as, clothed with spiritual bodies, they are conformed to the body of Christ's glory (2 Cor. 5:1-4; 1 Cor. 15:42ff.; Phil. 3:20f.). Yet even now, as they await this great and ultimate transformation, they are said to share in the first resurrection. Plainly, therefore, there is a resurrection that precedes the general resurrection. And the New Testament does indeed have much to say about another, earlier resurrection, itself an event of the greatest possible moment — the resurrection, namely, of Jesus from the dead. This is the only other resurrection, and it is well qualified to be designated "the first resurrection." (The miraculous restoration to life of some persons, such as the son of the widow of Nain and Lazarus, while significant of the power of God to raise the dead, is a lesser and temporary kind of resurrection, since for such persons it means a return to this present earthly life, only, sooner or later, to die again.) Christ's resurrection is the first resurrection not only in point of time but also in point of significance; for, as Paul says, "Christ has been raised from the dead, the first fruits of those who have fallen asleep" (1 Cor. 15:20). His rising is the guarantee and the dynamic cause of the second resurrection. It is the gage of the full harvest. It is the assurance to his followers that the same power of God that raised him will also raise them to eternal life and glory (2 Cor. 4:14), and to his despisers, conversely, that they will be raised to judgment and destruction (Acts 17:31).

Christian believers share in the blessedness of this first resurrection. Through faith and by God's grace they become one with Christ; and so intimate is this identification that his destiny becomes their destiny. This is the deep significance of Christian baptism: his resurrection from the dead is our resurrection from the dead, even now in this present life, and even in the interval between physical death and the glorification of the second resurrection. In baptism we are not only buried with Christ, but are "also raised with him through faith in the working of God, who raised him from the dead" (Col. 2:12). Similarly, Paul tells the Romans: "We were buried with him by baptism into death, so that as Christ was raised from the dead by the glory of the Father, we too might walk in newness of life" (Rom. 6:4). And, highly significant in the light of John's vision of the souls of believers living and reigning on thrones with Christ, there is the assertion, which could hardly be plainer, that God "raised us up with him, and made us sit with him [on thrones!] in the heavenly places in Christ Jesus" (Eph. 2:6; cf. Col. 3:1).

Wonderful as the reality of this union with Christ is for the believer here and now while he is still on earth, it is still more wonderful when, at death, he departs in his soul to be with Christ and finds himself exalted and enthroned in his presence. Here, crucially, is a still greater proof of the blessing that flows from that first resurrection and the evidence that the Christian truly has a share in it; for he now, through his own death, experiences the great truth that in Christ the sting of death and its fear have been removed (1 Cor. 15:56f.; Heb. 2:14f.), and finds that to be at home with Christ, though away from the body, is "far better" (2 Cor. 5:8; Phil. 1:23). Blessed, indeed, and holy is he who shares in the first resurrection! But most wonderful of all will be the moment of Christ's return at the end of this age, when in the second resurrection soul and body (now glorified) will be reunited, and in the fulness of his humanity the Christian believer will at last be totally and everlastingly conformed to the glorious image of the Son (Rom. 8:29; 1 Cor. 15:49; 2 Cor. 3:18; Phil. 3:21; 1 Jn. 3:2). Thus the full harvest of which the first resurrection is a surety will be brought in.

ONE THOUSAND YEARS

Our investigation of the hermeneutical principles by which the apostolic authors of the New Testament were guided in their interpretation of prophecy has led us to the following conclusions: (1) that this gospel era is the last age before the second coming of Christ; (2) that this age is, for believers, the age of responsibility for worldwide evangelism and, for the unregenerate, the age of opportunity for calling upon the name of the Lord; (3) that Christ is now enthroned as Lord at the right hand of the Father on high; (4) that this is his millennial reign and he must rule until every enemy has been subdued; (5) that he will then deliver the kingdom to God the Father, so that God may be all in all; and (6) that it is then that he will come again to judge the impenitent, to raise and receive those who are his to glory, and to establish the new heaven and the new earth (of which we shall have more to say shortly).

Those who insist on a literalistic principle of interpretation — though it is a principle to which even they find it impossible to adhere with consistency — object that "one thousand years" means what it says. If this is correct, then our understanding of Revelation 20 is clearly invalidated, because now nearly two millennia have passed by since Christ's ascension. But there is a variety of literary genres in the Bible — such as history, poetry, parable, and apocalyptic — and a proper respect for the text must take this consideration into account. To interpret literalistically what is intended symbolically cannot fail to do violence to the sacred text. Now the literary genre of the Revelation of John is that of apocalyptic, which accordingly by its very nature is a writing permeated with symbolical language. Occasionally, indeed, an interpretation is given of some of the symbolical elements of a vision, as, for example, where John describes the "one like a son of man" whom he saw standing in the midst of "seven golden lampstands" and holding in his right hand "seven stars" and the explanation is given that "the seven stars are the angels of the seven churches and the seven lampstands are the seven churches," though other details of the vision — such as the extreme whiteness of this "son of man's" hair and the likeness of his feet to "burnished bronze, refined as in a furnace" — are left for the reader to solve (Rev. 1:12-20). In the letters to the seven churches various blessings are promised to those who overcome: for example, that they will be given "some of the hidden manna," "a white stone," "the morning star," or will be made "pillars" in God's temple (2:17, 28; 3:12); but justice can be done to the text only if such terminology is understood symbolically. And this holds good for so much else in this book; though it is not necessary to assign a precise significance to every detail, since the effect is often cumulative, each particular contributing to the richness and splendor of the whole scene. Thus we read of one seated on a throne who "appeared like jasper and carnelian" and that "round the throne was a rainbow that looked like an emerald," while "before the throne burn seven torches of fire, which are the seven spirits of God," and on either side of it are "four living creatures" with the distinctive features of a lion, an ox, a man, and an eagle respectively, "each of them with six wings" and "full of eyes all round and within" (4:22ff.). In the same breath the glorified Redeemer is called "the Lion of the tribe of Judah" and "the Root of David" (5:5; cf. 22:16); but frequently this "Lion" is referred to as "the Lamb" (5:6, 8, 12, 13, etc.).

What could be more graphically symbolical than the "locusts" of chapter 9, which in appearance were "like horses arrayed for battle," with "what looked like crowns of gold on their heads," and with faces "like human faces" and hair "like women's hair" and "teeth like lions' teeth" and "scales like iron breastplates" and "tails like scorpions" and "stings" possessing "the power of hurting men for five months in their tails" (9:3ff.)? or, in chapter 12, the "great portent" of "a woman clothed with the sun, with the moon under her feet, and on her head a crown of twelve stars," and the further "portent" of "a great red dragon, with seven heads and ten horns, and seven diadems upon his heads" (12:1, 3)? or "the woman" portrayed in chapter 17 as "arrayed in purple and scarlet and bedecked with gold and jewels and pearls, holding in her hand a golden cup full of abominations and the impurities of her fornication," and written on her forehead "a name of mystery, 'Babylon the great, mother of harlots and of earth's abominations'" (17:3ff.)? Like other apocalyptic books, the Revelation of John is full of the cryptic and mysterious language of symbolism. However much one may be committed to a literalistic principle of interpretation, there is no possibility that the key of literalism will open the secrets of such symbolism; and, in practice even if not in theory, this fact is universally recognized by exponents of this book.

This being so, it is true no less of the **numbers** of the Revelation which are an integral component of the book's symbolism. Most prominent of all is the number **seven,** which recurs throughout the book. Thus we read of seven churches and seven spirits (1:4, etc.), seven lampstands (1:12, etc.), seven stars (1:16, etc.), seven torches of fire (4:5), seven seals (5:1, etc.), the Lamb with seven horns and seven eyes (5:6), seven angels and seven trumpets (8:2), seven thunders (10:3f.), seven angels with seven plagues (15:1ff.), seven golden bowls full of the wrath of God (15:7, etc.), and of the dragon and the beast, each of which has seven heads (12:3; 13:1, etc.). Of other numbers that are present it is sufficient to mention "the number of the beast" which is "a human number," namely, "six hundred and sixty-six," and which the reader "who has understanding" is invited to "reckon" or "work out" (13:18). This number is symbolical or it is nothing.

So also with the "thousands" of the book of Revelation. Mere consistency in interpretation demands that they too should be understood in a symbolical sense, whether it be the one hundred and forty-four thousand (or twelve times twelve thousand) who are sealed with the mark of God on their foreheads (7:2ff.; 14:1ff.), or the seven thousand who are killed in an earthquake (11:13), or the twelve thousand stadia which is the measure of the length, breadth, and height of the new Jerusalem (21:16), or the thousand years of chapter 20. As this is not intended to develop into a dissertation on the symbolism of numbers, we must be content to suggest here that this period of "one thousand years" symbolizes a period of time that is full but with limits which, in accordance with the sovereign will of God, are precisely defined, and that the fulness of this period of time coincides with the attainment of "the fulness of the Gentiles" and "the fulness of Israel," of which we have written above (pp. 89ff.). In other words, it is the period of these "last days" designated by God for the completion of all his purposes of grace and judgment; and it will be followed by the dawning of that day which has no evening, the unending sabbath of "the saints' everlasting rest." Such endless bliss it is beyond the power of number to symbolize.

CLIMAX OR ANTICLIMAX?

Despite the teaching of the apostles that "the end of all things is at hand" since it is upon us who live in this gospel era that "the ends of the ages have come" (1 Pet. 4:7; 1 Cor. 10:11), the advocates of premillennialism prefer to think otherwise, maintaining that the present (church) age, far from being the "last hour," will be followed by further periods or dispensations of which the most important will be the millennial age. They look forward to the millennium, when they expect Christ to reign on earth for one thousand years, as the climactic age of human history. In this way, they contend, the necessity for Christ to demonstrate his sovereign lordship over the whole earth will be satisfied, for this golden age of a thousand years will be an age of universal peace, prosperity, and justice during which Christ will rule the world with a rod of iron—otherwise, it is said, the world would never know what it is to be under the total dominion of Christ.

There will, however, be "the shadows of the millennium," to borrow an expression from a contemporary premillennial author; and these "shadows" can have only an invalidating effect on the alleged purpose of the millennial reign, indicating as they do that the total dominion of Christ in this period is more apparent than real and that it leads at last to a situation of incredible anticlimax. The millennial kingdom, in short, will be totalitarian rather than total and it will end in a massive rebellion of the forces of antichristianity. Submerged beneath the calm surface of this kingdom, we are told, sin will still persist in many hearts. On any who openly display their recalcitrance the severest punishment will be inflicted. But such challenges to the authority of the King will be incidental, and it is only at the conclusion of the thousand years that the hostility, no longer latent, bursts forth, as an army, whose number is like the sand of the sea (Rev. 20:8), is mobilized under the command of Satan.

Though the participants in this final insurrection are consumed by fire from heaven and thereupon brought to judgment before the great white throne and condemned to the lake of fire and brimstone, the mutiny of the nations at the conclusion of the millennial period makes nonsense of the supposed purpose of the thousand years' reign, namely, to establish the absolute supremacy of Christ as sovereign ruler on earth. Indeed, "the shadows of the millennium" then prove to have been cast by dark and terrible storm clouds which shut out the brightness of the sun above and cause all to end (so far as the alleged objective of the millennium is concerned) in anticlimax.

But it must also be said that "the shadows of the millennium," when it is interpreted in accordance with the presuppositions of the premillennialist, are cast by things long past as well as by things yet future. Of this we shall give but one example, namely, the expectation that the Jewish temple will be rebuilt in Jerusalem and the levitical sacrifices reinstituted. This expectation is closely tied to a literalistic principle of the interpretation of prophecy (though it is only fair to add that, while it is insisted on by virtually all dispensationalists, this belief is not universal among those whose viewpoint is premillennial). The attempt to justify it is based in the main on the prophecy contained in chapters 40-48 of Ezekiel which, it is contended, awaits literal fulfilment and will be literally fulfilled in the millennial kingdom.

In these chapters, written at a time when city and temple lay in ruins and the prophet himself was a victim of the Babylonian captivity, Ezekiel describes a vision he saw of a great temple built on a very high mountain in the land of Israel. The measurements of the temple and its precincts and the regulations for its priesthood and sacrifices are set down in great detail. The dimensions of the new city, which belongs to the same vision, are also given. It is of interest that the temple is not placed within the city, but stands on its own — though both stand on the royal and sacred territory which is in the center of the land and to the north and south of which are the territories allocated to the twelve tribes together with the aliens who have found a home in their midst and have become "as native-born sons of Israel" and fellow heirs of the promises (Ezek. 47:21-23). The city, moreover, has twelve gates, three on each of its four sides which are all of equal length, and each of the gates is named after one of the twelve tribes of Israel (48:15ff., 30ff.). Issuing from the temple the prophet sees an inexhaustible river of water which brings life wherever it flows and on either side of which are trees whose fruit, fresh every month, is for food and whose leaves, never wilting, are for healing (47:1ff.).

These are some of the outstanding features of this prophetic vision. The question is whether they are intended to receive a literal or a symbolical interpretation. The possibility of identifying Ezekiel's temple with the earlier temple of Solomon or the later and less impressive temple of Zerubbabel is ruled out by the specifications given in the vision. Accordingly, a fulfilment that is future rather than past seems to be demanded. The fact, however, that throughout the book of Ezekiel there is so much detailed and graphic imagery makes it intrinsically unlikely that the prophet's vision of the temple is meant to be interpreted in a literal manner. Once again, the distinctive nature or genre of the writing has to be taken into account.

Nonetheless, a literalistic approach to the text is characteristic, as we have said, of certain premillennialists, and this has led them to the conclusion that the temple of Ezekiel's vision will be built in the millennial age. The specifications given in the prophecy, moreover, concern not only the dimensions of the structure but also the worship that is to be conducted in it, and this worship is precisely that of the levitical sacrificial system. Consequently, the literalist has the further expectation that in connection with this millennial temple there will be a revival of the levitical priesthood and of the repetitious routine of the offering up of animal victims in sacrifice, including the blood-shedding associated with such sacrifice. But this would involve a reversion to Judaism, a turning back to a system that has long since served its intended purpose and been set aside; and the temptation to regress from the substance to the shadow is one against which the apostolic authors of the New Testament most insistently warn.

The restoration of the Old Testament sacrificial system would run clean counter to the emphatic teaching of the New Testament that the levitical order of priesthood has been abolished and that now the only priesthood is that of the order of Melchizedek, with but one priest, our Saviour Jesus Christ, who because he continues forever is a priest forever, and but one sacrifice, that offered by him once for all on the cross, with the result that there can be no further sacrifice for sin and no redeeming blood other than the blood he shed for us at Calvary (see pp. 76ff. above). It is no satisfactory rejoinder to assert that the millennial sacrifices will not be offered as **atoning** sacrifices but only as **commemorative** of the one perfect sacrifice; for if commemoration were necessary it would be effected by means of the ceremony instituted by Christ himself in commemoration of his saving sacrifice, that is to say, the sacrament of holy communion. But people do not commemorate one who is present with them, and, according to premillennialists, Christ will be personally present during his earthly reign of a thousand years, and present, what is more, with the marks of his suffering and death visible to all. This being so, it does not make sense to talk of commemoration.

The reinstitution of the levitical system would be an anticlimax of colossal proportions; but, worse than that, it would be contrary to the true essence of the Gospel and a disastrous return to the shadowy and temporary ordinances which have been irrevocably superseded by the perfection of the everlasting reality to which they pointed. It is futile to attempt to place the new wine of the Gospel in the old wineskins!

THE NEW HEAVEN AND THE NEW EARTH

There is, however, another way of understanding the significance of Ezekiel's temple vision which is in harmony with the context of the millennial passage in Revelation 20 and, indeed, with the principles by which the apostolic writers interpret the ancient prophecies elsewhere in the New Testament. Ezekiel and Revelation have this in common, too, that they are both apocalyptic writings in which particular visions are recorded. But we may go further and state that in many respects the book of Revelation provides a key to the understanding of the prophecy of Ezekiel. This we shall now hope to demonstrate.

First, the reference to **Gog and Magog** in Revelation 20:7ff. is taken over directly from Ezekiel (chs. 38 and 39). John describes this part of his vision in the following terms:

> And when the thousand years are ended, Satan will be loosed from his prison and will come out to deceive the nations which are at the four corners of the earth, that is, Gog and Magog, to gather them for battle; their number is like the sand of the sea. And they marched up over the broad earth and surrounded the camp of the saints and the beloved city; but fire came down from heaven and consumed them.

It is plain that this final act of defiance takes place in the "little period" (Rev. 20:3) when Satan is unloosed at the conclusion of the thousand years and resumes his activity as the deceiver of the nations, and that it is immediately followed by the judgment of the great white throne and the inauguration of the new heaven and the new earth (Rev. 20:11ff.; 21:1ff.). In the vision of Ezekiel the insurrection of Gog and Magog, upon whose hosts the destruction of "torrential rain and hailstones, fire and brimstone" is sent, is followed by the vision of the new temple and the new city. From

131

this sequence of events it is only reasonable to conclude that (in John's mind at least) the temple and city of Ezekiel have a close correspondence with the new heaven and the new earth of the Revelation. Premillennialists, however, disregard the significance of this sequence in Ezekiel's prophecy.

Secondly, as in Ezekiel so also in the Revelation the seer is shown the city by an angel who has a measuring rod with which he measures the city's dimensions (Ezek. 40:3; 48:15ff.; Rev. 21:15). The detailed measurements indicate the preciseness of God's designs and their execution; the shape of the city as a perfect square (indeed, in John's Revelation, a perfect cube) signifies the perfection of these designs; and the magnitude of its proportions reflects the vastness of God's grace and goodness (cf. Rev. 7:9; 21:24-26). The correspondence is further confirmed by the fact that in both visions the city has twelve gates, three on each of the four sides, and that the twelve gates are named after the twelve tribes of Israel (Ezek. 48:30ff.; Rev. 21:12f.).

Thirdly, it should be remarked that as in Ezekiel the temple is not in the city so also John says: "I saw no temple in the city, for its temple is the Lord God the Almighty, even the Lamb" (Rev. 21:22).

Fourthly, the abundant river of water which Ezekiel sees flowing from the temple of God and bringing life wherever it goes, and on whose banks grow trees bearing fruit every month and unfading leaves for food and healing (Ezek. 47:1ff.), is beautifully matched and fulfilled by the vision given to John, who writes:

> Then he showed me the river of the water of life, bright as crystal, flowing from the throne of God and of the Lamb through the middle of the street of the city; also, on either side of the river, the tree of life with its twelve kinds of fruit, yielding its fruit each month; and the leaves of the tree were for the healing of the nations (Rev. 22:1f.).

132

These prophecies, then, are descriptive of the state of blessedness which will prevail universally and everlastingly in the new heaven and the new earth, following the final destruction of Satan and his followers. The conception of "the new heaven and the new earth" denotes the renewal of God's creation and the fulfilment of the purpose for which God brought the created order into being. "Heaven and earth" as a designation of the totality of creation is an echo of the opening words of the book of Genesis, where we read: "In the beginning God created the heavens and the earth" (Gen. 1:1). Furthermore, it should be noticed that the glorious and eternal future that is envisaged includes **the earth.** It is not an ethereal or nebulous future that is promised to God's people; for "the earth is the Lord's and the fulness thereof" (Ps. 24:1), and God did not make all things in order to watch them end in destruction and futility. That is why Paul speaks of the creation, at present "subjected to futility," as "waiting with eager longing" for the day when "it will be set free from its bondage to decay and obtain the glorious liberty of the children of God" (Rom. 8:18-21). In the transcendental sphere also the Lord God is praised as worthy to receive glory and honor and power on the ground that he is the Creator of all things and that it was by his will that they were brought into existence (Rev. 4:11).

The glorious future promised to God's people, therefore, is a glorious future also for the whole created order — of which, let us not forget, man is a part, indeed the crowning part. Just as the fall of man brought a curse upon the rest of creation, so also the exaltation of man to his true destiny in Christ will mean the restoration of the whole order of creation to the perfection with which it was marked when it issued from the hand of God. This is the significance of "the new heaven and the new earth," over which the divine lordship will be not be forced and superficial but universally welcome and thorough, and not for a thousand years but for evermore. As the conclusion of the book of the Revelation so plainly shows, it is with the return of Christ to judge the world, and to bring in that eternal age of blessedness for which the whole creation yearns, that the prophecy of Isaiah concerning a new heaven and a new earth, in which the wolf dwells with the lamb and the leopard with the kid and none shall hurt or destroy in all God's holy mountain because "the earth shall be full of the knowledge of the Lord as the waters cover the sea," will find its everlasting fulfilment (Is. 65:17ff.; 11:6ff.; cf. Hab. 2:14).

Meanwhile in this age of the Gospel the power of that kingdom and the reality of that blessedness are tasted within the fellowship of the redeemed as they "press on toward the goal for the prize of the upward call in Christ Jesus," their gaze fixed on "the day of Jesus Christ," that great day when God will bring to completion that good work he has begun in them (Phil. 3:14; 1:6). On that day all God's covenant promises will be brought to full and everlasting fruition, in accordance with the proclamation from the throne which John heard in his vision:

> "Behold, the dwelling of God is with men. He will dwell with them, and they shall be his people, and God himself will be with them; he will wipe away every tear from their eyes, and death shall be no more, neither shall there be mourning nor crying nor pain any more, for the former things have passed away" (Rev. 21:3f.).

No longer cut off from the tree of life and from the river of the water of life, and no longer excluded from the presence and the blessing of God (Gen. 2:9f.; 3:24), the curse which man's sin brought on the world will be fully removed, never to return:

> There shall no more be anything accursed, but the throne of God and of the Lamb shall be in it ["the city of the living God, the heavenly Jerusalem," Heb. 12:22], and his servants shall worship him; they

134

shall see his face, and his name shall be on their foreheads. And night shall be no more; they need no light of lamp or sun, for the Lord God will be their light, and they shall reign for ever and ever (Rev. 22:3ff.).

This is our indescribably wonderful heritage in Christ Jesus, and it is toward this glorious consummation that this present age is moving — this age of the Gospel in which the Holy Spirit is preparing the church of those who have been cleansed and sanctified to be presented to Christ in glory as his bride, "without spot or wrinkle or any such thing, . . . holy and without blemish" (Eph. 5:25-27). Until the Bridegroom comes, this is still the age of gospel invitation, in which "the Spirit and the Bride say, 'Come,'" and he who is athirst is urged to drink the water of life freely (Rev. 22:17), and in which those who love and long for the Bridegroom's appearing hear his words of reassurance, "Surely I am coming soon," and respond with all their hearts, "Come, Lord Jesus!" (Rev. 22:20).